SCM PAPERBACKS
by William Barclay

THE MIND OF JESUS

CRUCIFIED AND CROWNED

NEW TESTAMENT WORDS

THE MASTER'S MEN

PRAYERS FOR THE CHRISTIAN YEAR

EPILOGUES AND PRAYERS

LETTERS TO THE SEVEN CHURCHES

THE LORD'S SUPPER

D1426807

WILLIAM BARCLAY

Crucified and Crowned

SCM PRESS LTD
BLOOMSBURY STREET LONDON

334 00274 5

First published 1961
by SCM Press Ltd
56 Bloomsbury Street London
Second impression 1963
Third impression 1967
Fourth impression 1971
Fifth impression 1974
Sixth impression 1976

Printed in Great Britain by
Fletcher & Son Ltd, Norwich

CONTENTS

To
the Members of the
Twelve Club

*

*Iron sharpens iron,
and one man sharpens another*
PROVERBS 27.17

PREFACE

As in the case of its predecessor, *The Mind of Jesus*, the substance of this book first appeared as a series of weekly articles in the pages of the *British Weekly*, and I am most grateful to the Rev. Denis Duncan, the editor of that weekly, for his kind permission to republish that material in book form. But it is true that the material has been so extensively rewritten, and so much has been added, that the book in many places bears little relationship to the original articles.

Anyone who writes about the death of Jesus, about the Cross and its meaning, about the things to come, must have at the back of his mind a very strange feeling. He is conscious that he is writing about the greatest things in all the world, and yet he is conscious that all the time he is walking in a realm of controversy, a battle-ground of opposing theologies, an area in which the words heretic, liberal, radical, modernist, conservative, fundamentalist have been hurled by one set of thinkers at another. In such circumstances there seems to me only one thing to do. I think that a man, without disregarding and without attacking the beliefs of others, must witness to his own. Certain of the things I have written in this book will certainly seem to others to be wrong and mistaken, but I can only say that this is what I believe and this is how there came into my life the new relationship to God which is the very essence of the Christian faith and of the work of Jesus Christ. 'There are as many ways to the stars as there are men to climb them,' and what may seem to another wrong and dangerous has been right and precious to me.

This book has many debts, and I have tried to acknowledge them in their own places. I should like particularly to acknowledge two debts in connection with the chapter entitled 'Looking at the Cross.' In that chapter I have drawn largely on David Smith's *The Atonement in the Light of History and the Modern Spirit* and on H. E. W. Turner's *The Patristic Doctrine of Redemption.* It is not so much that I have been in any way dependent on the thought and the conclusions of these books as that I have allowed myself freely to draw on the material which they provide, although I have always checked and investigated that material in its original sources.

Once again I would like to set down my thanks to the Rev. David L. Edwards, the Editor of the SCM Press, for constant kindness, wise criticism and guidance. And I would be sadly lacking in courtesy if I did not express my thanks to Miss Jean Cunningham, also of the SCM Press, for her work in the preparation of my manuscript for printing. Her meticulous and scholarly checking of references and correcting of errors has saved this book from many faults, and has caused her and saved me many hours of labour.

I shall be well content if this book does something to enable its readers, not to argue about Jesus and his work, but to see a little more of the love of God in him.

Trinity College,　　　　　　　WILLIAM BARCLAY
Glasgow

ACKNOWLEDGEMENTS

'THE Donkey' by G. K. Chesterton is quoted from *The Wild Knight and other poems*, published by J. M. Dent, by permission of Miss D. E. Collins.

'To and Fro About the City' by John Drinkwater is quoted from his *Collected Poems*, Vol. II, published by Sidgwick and Jackson, by permission of the publisher.

1

THE APPEAL OF A ROYAL LOVE

THE road to Jerusalem was a road which it was not easy for Jesus to take; no man ever looked forward to death in the agony of a cross. Luke says of him: 'When the days drew near for him to be received up, he set his face to go to Jerusalem' (Luke 9.51). His face looked as if it had been carved in granite; his countenance bore the mark of the inner struggle and determination of his soul. Mark with a vivid touch describes the last journey. 'And they were on the road, going up to Jerusalem, and Jesus was walking ahead of them; and they were amazed, and those who followed were afraid' (Mark 10.32). Jesus was walking out in front of them, and for once there was something about him which made them hesitate to intrude upon that loneliness in which he was enveloped. This was a road which Jesus had to walk alone, and he had to compel himself to walk it.

What awaited him at Jerusalem? In Jerusalem it was Passover time, the time which Jesus had deliberately chosen for the climax and the culmination of his work on earth.

The city was crowded to its utmost capacity; not only from all over Palestine but also from all over the world Jews thronged to keep the Passover. Josephus tells how Nero was contemptuous of the Jewish nation. Cestius, the governor of Palestine during part of Nero's reign, wished to convince him of the importance of the Jews. Cestius, therefore, requested the priests to take a count of the number of Jews who came to Jerusalem to observe the Passover. Every

Passover lamb had to be slain and the blood of it sacrificed in the Temple courts. So the priests took their count by counting the number of the Passover lambs. The number of lambs slain was 256,500. The minimum number for a celebration of the Passover was ten, but, as Josephus points out, there could be as many as twenty in a Passover company; so Josephus reckons the number of Passover pilgrims as about 2,700,200 people.[1] It was into a city crowded like that that Jesus came. He could not have chosen to come to Jerusalem at a time when the crowds were greater or the religious feeling more intense.

When Jesus came into Jerusalem, he walked straight into the midst of his enemies. It may well be true that by this time Jesus was an outlaw with a price upon his head. John tells of the ways in which the people discussed whether or not Jesus would come to the Passover, and then goes on to say: 'Now the chief priests and the Pharisees had given orders that if anyone knew where Jesus was, he should let them know, so that they might arrest him' (John 11.56f.). When Jesus came into Jerusalem, he was in the eyes of the authorities a criminal marked down for arrest.

In view of that it would have been common prudence to have stayed away from Jerusalem altogether, or at least to have slipped in unseen and to lie concealed and to keep to the back streets. That is precisely what Jesus did not do. Jesus' decision to come into Jerusalem in such a way that every eye should be focused upon him was no sudden decision of impulse; it was deliberate, and the means to do so had been arranged far ahead. He sent his disciples ahead to find the ass on which he was to ride into the city. This was something which he had long ago arranged with some friend whose name we will never know. If anyone questioned their right to take the animal, they were to say: 'The Lord has need of it,' which was clearly a prearranged signal and pass-

[1] *Wars of the Jews* 6.9.3.

word (Mark 11.2f.; Luke 19.30f.; Matt. 21.2f.). So they brought the ass, and Jesus came riding into Jerusalem, into the midst of the crowds, and into the hands of the enemies who had determined to destroy him. Even if we were to go no further, we should be bound to say that this entry of Jesus into Jerusalem was an act of supreme courage. There is a courage which is born of the impulse of the moment, a courage born at some sudden emergency in which a man has no time to think, and in which he becomes a hero by a kind of instinctive reaction. But there is an even higher courage, the courage of the man who has had long to think, the courage of the man who sees with complete clarity the terrible things which lie ahead, and who deliberately, of set purpose and having counted the cost, goes on. That is the highest of all kinds of courage, and that was the courage of Jesus when he entered Jerusalem.

When Jesus rode into Jerusalem, he used a method of action which many a prophet of Israel had used. The prophets had often used the method of dramatic and symbolic action. Men might refuse to listen, but men could hardly fail to see; and again and again the prophets had cast their message into the form of some vivid action, as if to say: 'If you will not listen, you must *see*.' It was thus that Ahijah foretold to Jeroboam that ten tribes would revolt to him and that two would remain with Rehoboam, by tearing the new garment into twelve pieces and handing ten of them to him (I Kings 11.29-40). It was thus that Jeremiah forewarned the people of the slavery that was to fall upon them, by making yokes and wearing them on his neck, and it was thus that the false prophet deceivingly foretold that the slavery would not happen, by taking and breaking the yokes Jer. 27.1-11; 28.10f.). This method of dramatic and symbolic action was one of Ezekiel's favourite ways of delivering his message (Ezek. 4 and 5). Jesus in his entry into Jerusalem was putting his message into the form of a dramatic, sym-

bolic, meaningful, significant action, for a message can enter
by eye-gate when ear-gate is closed, and a message delivered
to the eye can reach many more than a message delivered to
the ear. What, then, was this message of Jesus?

It was a deliberately made claim to be king. No doubt
Jesus was remembering the prophecy of Zechariah which
Matthew cites: 'Behold your king is coming to you . . .
mounted on an ass' (Zech. 9.9; Matt. 21.5). It is easy for
a Western mind completely to misread this action of Jesus.
G. K. Chesterton wrote his poem about the donkey:

> When fishes flew and forests walk'd
>   And figs grew upon thorn,
> Some moment when the moon was blood
>   Then surely I was born.
>
> With monstrous head and sickening cry
>   And ears like errant wings,
> The devil's walking parody
>   Of all four-footed things.
>
> The tatter'd outlaw of the earth,
>   Of ancient crooked will;
> Starve, scourge, deride me: I am dumb,
>   I keep my secret still.
>
> Fools! For I also had my hour,
>   One far fierce hour and sweet:
> There was a shout about my ears,
>   And palms before my feet.

It is a magnificent poem, but it is based on a misunderstanding. Nowadays in the West the ass is a beast of carica-
ture and fun; but in the East in the time of Jesus the ass was
a noble beast. In the ancient days Jair, who judged Israel,
had thirty sons who rode on thirty asses (Judg. 10.4), and
Abdon had forty sons and thirty grandsons who rode on
seventy asses (Judg. 12.14). The ass was the beast on which
kings rode when they came in peace; only in war did they

ride upon horses. The entry of Jesus was the claim to be King.

But at the same time it was the claim to be the King of peace. It was upon the ass of peace and not upon the horse of war that Jesus came. He came deliberately refusing the role of the warrior Messiah and claiming to be the Prince of peace. He was appealing for a throne, but the throne was in the hearts of men. In that entry into Jerusalem Jesus, in a dramatic symbolic action which spoke more loudly than any words, was making one last appeal to men, and saying to them: 'Will you not, even now, even yet, accept me as your Lord and King, and enthrone me within your hearts?'

Jesus' entry into Jerusalem was an action of supreme courage; it was an assertion of royalty and an offer of love; it was at one and the same time royalty's claim and love's appeal.

2

THE WRATH OF A PURE LOVE

WHEN Jesus entered Jerusalem, it was natural that the Temple should be the first place to which he should go. His first visit to it was late in the evening. He neither spoke nor acted, but, as Mark has it, he looked round at everything, and then he went out to Bethany with his disciples to spend the night there (Mark 11.11). On the next morning he came back to the Temple, and he proceeded to enact what may well be called the most spectacular event in his whole career, the event which we call the Cleansing of the Temple. He came into the Temple court, and he drove out all those who were selling and buying; he overturned the tables of the money-changers, and the seats of the sellers of victims for the sacrifices (Matt. 21.12; Mark 11.15; Luke 19.45), and, as Mark adds, he would not allow anyone to carry anything through the Temple (Mark 11.16). What was it that so aroused the wrath of Jesus and impelled him to an action of such unparalleled audacity?

Every adult, male, freeborn Jew, who was not a priest, had to pay a yearly Temple tax of half-a-shekel. It is difficult, if not impossible, to give the exact equivalent of any ancient coin; and in seeking to understand money equivalents in terms of modern values, it has to be remembered that the sums have to be multiplied twenty or thirty times to find the equivalent modern purchasing power. However, a shekel is usually said to be equivalent to one shilling and twopence; but that sum is to be evaluated against the fact that in

Palestine a working man's wage for a day's work was about eightpence; and, therefore, the Temple tax was not far short of two days' wages. It is calculated that this Temple tax brought in about £75,000 a year. The extraordinary wealth of the Temple may be seen from the fact that, when Crassus plundered it during his expedition to the East in 54–53 B.C., he took from it money and gold to the value of at least £2,500,000.[1] The payment of the Temple tax was obligatory, and, if it was not paid, it was legally possible for the Temple authorities to distrain upon a defaulter's goods.

Intimation that the Temple tax was due was made on the first day of the month Adar, the month immediately before the month of Nisan in which the Passover fell. On the fifteenth day of Adar, exactly a month before the Passover, stalls were set up in all the towns and villages, and at them the Temple tax could be paid. These stalls remained open until the twenty-fifth day of Adar. Thereafter the Temple tax could be paid only in the Temple itself.

The Temple consisted of a series of courts.[2] There was first the Court of the Gentiles into which anyone of any nation could come, and beyond that court no Gentile could pass on pain of death. Next, there came the Court of the Women, beyond which no woman could pass, unless she was on actual sacrificial business. Next, there was the Court of the Israelites, at the rail of which the offerings of the worshippers were handed over to the priests. Next, there was the Court of the Priests into which only the priests could go, and where the altar of the burnt-offering stood. Finally, at the far end of the Court of the Priests there was the Holy Place, the Temple building proper, and at the west end of this, behind a veil, the Holy of Holies, into which only the High Priest might go, and he only on the Day of Atonement.

---

[1]   Josephus, *Antiquities of the Jews* 14.7.1; *Wars of the Jews* 1.8.8.
[2]   Josephus, *Against Apion* 2.8.

In the time of Jesus the Court of the Gentiles had become far more like a crowded, noisy, huckstering market than the approach to the house of God. It was there that the money-changers had their stalls and tables. The necessity for the money-changers lay in the fact that the Temple tax had to be paid in certain kinds of currency and in no others. All kinds of coins of silver, Roman, Greek, Syrian, Phoenician, Persian, Tyrian, were current and valid for all ordinary purposes in Palestine; but the Temple tax had to be paid either in half-shekels of the sacred standard, or in Galilaean shekels. One Galilaean shekel was equal in value to one half-shekel of the sacred standard. The reason why these currencies alone were valid was that they had no king's head stamped on them. Other currencies bore a king's head, and were, therefore, graven images and unclean for sacred purposes. As we have said, for all normal purposes a wide variety of currencies was valid. And, further, Jews came from all over the world from many countries to keep the Passover, bringing with them the money of the country from which they came. The function of the money-changers was to change the money of the pilgrims into the only kinds of coins which were acceptable to the Temple authorities. On the face of it it was a useful enough function; but it had been turned into an imposition and a major financial ramp. For every coin which was changed the money-changers charged a fee of one *maah*, a coin worth about twopence; and, if the coin to be changed was of greater value than a half-shekel, the person who offered it was compelled to pay another *maah* in order to receive the change from it. That is to say, many and many a pilgrim had to pay not only his half-shekel Temple tax, but a sum of fourpence extra in order to get the right coin and his change from his own money. And it must again be remembered that this fourpence has to be evaluated in light of the fact that a working-man's wage for a day's work was about eightpence. It took him half a day's wages to obtain the right coin and to receive his change. This money-changing tax was called *quolbon*, and it has been estimated that it brought in between £8000 and £9000 a year. What was little better than a gigantic financial swindle was being worked on poor pilgrims who could ill afford it. The matter was often complicated by the fact that the silver of the coins offered was worn and the coins were thin; they were then weighed, and there was further grasping and acrimonious dispute as to their true value.

In addition to the money-changers, the sellers of pigeons and doves had their booths in the Court of the Gentiles. A great many pilgrims wished to make an offering of thanksgiving. Apart from the offering of the special thanksgiving a great many routine offerings had to be made. For instance, after childbirth a woman had to offer either a lamb and a pigeon, or, if she was too poor to do so, two pigeons (Lev. 12.6-8). Of course, such offerings could be bought in shops outside the Temple; but the Temple authorities had their official inspectors whose duty it was to inspect all sacrificial victims to see that they were without spot or blemish and fit to be offered. If a victim was bought from an outside shop, it had to be submitted to an inspector, and a fee paid for its examination; and it was to all intents and purposes certain that the inspector would find a flaw, whereas the animals sold within the Temple courts had already been inspected. Again, on the face of it, it would seem that the booths which sold the animals within the Court of the Gentiles were fulfilling a useful enough purpose; but there had been occasions when a pair of doves cost as little as ninepence outside the Temple and as much as fifteen shillings within the Temple. The booths within the Temple charged prices which were an imposition on the pilgrims and on those who came to sacrifice. Still further, these booths were known as the Bazaars of Annas, and were the private business of the family of Annas, who had once been High Priest.

Mark alone has the addition that Jesus would not allow anyone to carry anything through the Temple (Mark 11.16). On this the Jewish law as contained in the *Mishnah* was quite clear. 'A man may not enter into the Temple mount with his staff or his sandal or his wallet, or with the dust upon his feet, nor may he make of it a short bypath; still less may he spit there' (*Berakoth* 9.5). Quite clearly the Jewish traders were breaking their own law in the way in which they used the Temple Court, and the Temple authorities were actually guilty of encouraging them to do so. And in the time of Jesus it was the common custom to use the Temple Court as a convenient short-cut from the city to the Mount of Olives.

It is not difficult to imagine the uproar, the disturbance, the disputing, the haggling, the bargaining, and the swindling which went on in the Court of the Gentiles. Anything less like the approach to the house of God would be difficult to imagine. What should have been what the prophet called 'a house of prayer for all nations' (Isa. 56.7) had become what Jeremiah called 'a den of robbers' (Jer. 7.11; Matt. 21.13; Mark 11.17; Luke 19.46).

In the action of the cleansing of the Temple the mind of Jesus is clearly revealed to us.

Here Jesus acts as nothing less than the spokesman of God. He did not cleanse the Temple like some church office-bearer or official attacking some abuse or cleaning up some evil and improper situation. He cleansed the Temple *as if it belonged to him*, as if it was his own personal house and dwelling-place. In this action and event Jesus did nothing less than identify his own action with the action of God. He does not act like a man dealing with some abuse; he acts like God sweeping the evil from his own house.

Here Jesus acts as nothing less than judge. In the vision of Ezekiel of the days when judgment was to come, the command was: 'Begin at my sanctuary' (Ezek. 9.6). In the action of the cleansing of the Temple Jesus assumed the right of judgment, and that judgment began at the sanctuary. Jesus' consciousness of authority is demonstrated for all to see, in that he was prepared to judge and to condemn those who were responsible for the administration and ordering of what to the Jews was nothing other than the House of God.

Here Jesus acts as nothing less than Messiah. The restoration of the Temple to an even greater glory was a regular part of the visions of the messianic age. The Book of Enoch looks to the day when the old house will be folded up, when its pillars and its ornaments will be carried away, and when a new house greater and loftier than the first will arise (Enoch 90.28f.). The Psalms of Solomon look forward to a day when Jerusalem shall be purged until she shall be holy as of old, and when the Lord shall be glorified in a place to be seen of all the earth (Psalms of Solomon 17.30). It was as if Jesus said: 'The day has come when the House of God shall be purified of those who defile it, for the Messiah has arrived in his own city.'

Jesus' ejection of the money-changers and the sellers of doves demonstrates his passion for social justice. His anger was kindled to a white heat at the sight of simple people cheated, swindled, imposed upon by clever and rapacious scoundrels. Here in this event is the affirmation of the social gospel which regards the exploitation of men as a crime against God.

There is an even deeper condemnation here; there is the condemnation of anything which hinders ordinary people in their search for God. Into the Court of the Gentiles all nations and all people might come. To the Passover there came not only Jews from all over the world, but also people from many other nations, for Jerusalem was one of the wonders of the world, which tourists came from all over to see. Many must have come to the Temple with a sense and hope that perhaps there they might find God; and instead they found a swaying, disputing, bargaining mob, and an atmosphere in which devotion was impossible. The place which should have been, as Mark had it, a house of prayer *for all nations* had become a market-place where avaricious traders swindled and shrewd tourists bargained. There are other ways than that of producing an atmosphere within a church in which it is very difficult for the simple seeker to find God, and any who render the search for God more difficult must face the anger of Jesus.

It may be that buried deep in the heart of this event there lies something which goes far beyond the moment in which it happened, yet something which may well have been in the heart and the mind of Jesus. It may well be that the deep and basic meaning of this event is that it was a condemnation of the whole apparatus of sacrifice and the whole ritual of the Temple. Jesus had long before this quoted God's word to Hosea: 'I desire mercy and not sacrifice' (Matt. 9.13; Hos. 6.6), and the driving of the money-changers and the sellers of victims from the Temple Court may well symbolically mean that all the sacrificial ritual for which they stood was a vast irrelevancy, which had no real place in the House of God. Animal sacrifice could never be a substitute for the offer of the heart's love to God and to man.

It only remains to remember something more simple and more elemental than any of these things. Like the triumphal entry—only, if possible, more so—the cleansing of the Temple was an act of sublime and magnificent courage. It was sheer and utter defiance. It may well be argued that the cleansing of the Temple was the Rubicon in the life of Jesus. In this action he burned his boats forever. He carried the war into the camp of the enemy; yet at the same time, by striking such a blow at the vested interests of trade and religion, humanly speaking, Jesus signed his own death-warrant—and he knew it.

3

THE THREAT OF A DEMANDING LOVE

It is only in the last week of his life that we can follow Jesus from day to day and almost from hour to hour. It was on the Sunday that he came riding into Jerusalem. It was on the Monday that he cleansed the Temple, driving out the money-changers and the sellers of sacrificial victims. The Tuesday was a day of concentrated controversy and teaching. On that day, according to the Gospel narrative, four deputations came to Jesus, each trying to trip and to entangle him in his words. The first demanded to know on what authority he acted as he did (Matt. 22.23-27; Mark 11.27-33; Luke 20.1-8). The second sought to inveigle him into making dangerous statements about the paying of the tribute money to Rome (Matt. 22.15-21; Mark 12.13-17; Luke 20.20-26). The third was the deputation of the Sadducees who sought to entangle him in questions about the life to come (Matt. 22.23-33; Mark 12.18-27; Luke 20.27-38). The fourth demanded that he should tell them which was the greatest of the commandments (Matt. 22.34-40; Mark 12.28-34). In each case Jesus dealt wisely with his questioners and defeated their evil intentions.

It was on this day also that Jesus, as Matthew tells the story, told a series of great parables—the parables of the two sons (Matt. 21.28-32); of the wedding feast (Matt. 22.1-14); of the ten virgins (Matt. 25.1-13); of the talents (Matt. 25.14-30); of the sheep and the goats (Matt. 25.31-46).

But there is one parable of that day which all the three

Gospel writers record, the parable of the wicked husbandmen (Matt. 21.33-46; Mark 12.1-12; Luke 20.9-18). In
their selection of the material available to them there were
things which each of the Gospel writers was willing to omit;
but so indelible was the imprint of this parable, and so
unforgettable was its effect, that all three without exception
record it. And it is right that it should be so, for in that
parable is the concentrated essence of the last days of Jesus'
life in the flesh upon earth. Seldom did he make so great a
claim, fling down so unmistakable a challenge, utter so
terrible a threat.

In Palestine men were very familiar with absentee land-
lords who did with their estates exactly what the owner of
the vineyard in the parable did. The owner of the vineyard
equipped his vineyard with the best possible equipment—a
thickset hedge to keep out the wild beasts, a watchtower to
keep guard against the marauders, a wine press where the
juice might be extracted from the grapes. He then let it out
to cultivators. There were in Palestine three possible arrangements about the payment of rent. The rent might be an
agreed sum of money; it might be an agreed and fixed
amount of produce; and it might be an agreed proportion of
the crop. The time came when the rent for the vineyard fell
due, and the owner sent his servants to collect it. One after
another the servants were maltreated, injured, beaten,
stoned, killed by the cultivators. Finally the owner sent his
son, thinking that the cultivators were bound to respect him;
but the cultivators took the son and killed him, and planned
to seize the vineyard for themselves. Then the owner of the
vineyard was compelled to act. He dealt out terrible and
deserved punishment to the cultivators and gave the vineyard to others.

We are always rightly warned that we must not turn the
parables of Jesus into allegories, that they teach one flashing
truth, and that the details are not to be pressed and not to

be provided each with a meaning. But in this one parable the case is different, for both the meaning of the whole parable and the meaning of the details are crystal clear. As both the prophets and the Psalmist had it: 'The vineyard of the Lord of hosts is the house of Israel' (Isa. 5.1-7; Jer. 2.21; Ps. 80.8). The vineyard is Israel. The cultivators into whose hands the vineyard was entrusted are the rulers and the leaders of Israel. The owner of the vineyard is God. The messengers are the prophets. It was the lament of Jesus that Jerusalem was the city which killed the prophets and stoned those who were sent unto her (Matt. 23.37). Later Stephen was to confront the Sanhedrin with the demand: 'Which of the prophets did not your fathers persecute?' (Acts 7.52). The threat of the parable is the threat that Israel's place of privilege is to be taken from her, and to be given to others— and those who heard the parable well understood it, for their shocked reaction was to say: 'God forbid!' (Luke 20.16). This is a parable which sheds a flood of light upon the mind of Jesus.

(i)   Here we find *the claim of Jesus*. In this parable Jesus deliberately removes himself from the succession of the prophets. Each in his day and generation they had brought his message, and then had often paid for their loyalty with their lives; but they were *servants*, while he is *the Son*. In this parable Jesus presents himself as the Son of God, come with God's last word, God's final invitation, God's ultimate appeal to Israel. The day of the prophet was past; the day of the Son had come. There were no further lengths to which the appeal and invitation of God could go.

(ii)   Here is *the courage of Jesus*. This parable makes it quite clear that Jesus knew that he was to die. His certainty of death to come was not the result of any miraculous fore-knowledge; anyone who could read the signs could see what was going to happen. The leaders and the rulers and the orthodox were out for his blood, and he knew it. Escape was still perfectly possible. It was not too late to effect a compromise with the rulers; it was not too late to slip out of Jerusalem and to get away from it all. But neither compromise nor flight ever entered Jesus' mind. Homer makes Achilles say, even when death was certain, 'Nevertheless, I am for going on.'[1] Jesus knew where his chosen pathway was leading—and yet he took it.

(iii)   Here is *the threat of Jesus*. The vineyard was to be taken and given to others. Here is a vivid and pictorial way of saying that Israel was to lose her place in God's scheme of things, that all her privilege in the plan of God was to be taken from her. The New Testament is clear that the new Israel is the Church. The Church is the Israel of God (Gal. 6.16). They are not all Israel which are of Israel; the racial descendants of Abraham are not all sons of Abraham in the true sense of the word (Rom. 9.6f.). It is faith, the same faith which Abraham showed, which makes a man a true son of Abraham and an heir of all the promises (Rom. 4.16). A man is not a true Jew who is only a Jew outwardly, and whose circumcision is nothing more than a mark in the flesh; true circumcision is circumcision of the heart, and the true Jew is the man who is a Jew inwardly (Rom. 2.28f.). It is those who are of faith who are the children of Abraham (Gal. 3.7). If a man is Christ's, then he is a true descendant of Abraham, and all the promises are his (Gal. 3.29). The Jews could never forget that they were the chosen people; but Jesus warned them that they were on their way to losing their position in the plan of God. And so it happened; the Christian Church became the new Israel; and the promises which once belonged to the Jews were transferred to it.

(iv)   Here is *the confidence of Jesus*. The end of the parable is the expression by Jesus of the confidence of triumph and vindication to come. For that picture he went to the Psalms. In the Psalms there is the picture of the stone

[1]   *Iliad* 18.114.

which the builders rejected but which in the end became the head of the corner (Ps. 118.22; cp. Acts 4.11; I Peter 2.4,7). That picture was originally meant to apply to the nation of Israel, but Jesus took it to himself to express his own confidence in his final triumph.

Here in this parable we see Jesus flinging down his challenge. He claims a unique relationship to God. He claims the right to judge and to condemn and to reject Israel. He is aware that the road he is taking will end upon the Cross. But never for one moment does he see the Cross as the end. He goes on in the certainty that beyond the Cross there lies the ultimate triumph.

4

THE ANOINTING OF LOVE

THE last week of Jesus' life was lived in a blaze of publicity, and in an atmosphere of conflict. On the Sunday he came riding into Jerusalem; on the Monday he cleansed the Temple, descending on men like the wrath of God; on the Tuesday he had repeatedly to meet those who came to him with questions, not because they were seeking for information and for guidance, but because they were seeking to entrap and to entangle him in his words. But on the Wednesday there came an oasis of sweetness in the desert of bitterness, for on that day there came to him one of the loveliest things which happened to him in all the days of his flesh, and on that day he received one of the last kindnesses which he was to receive at the hands of anyone in the days of his earthly life (Matt. 26.6-13; Mark 14.3-9).

On the Wednesday Jesus did not come into Jerusalem, but remained in the quietness of the village of Bethany. He was invited to a meal by a certain man known as Simon the leper. In Palestine a meal could be a very public occasion. The houses of the well-to-do were built round an open courtyard, in which there was often a garden and a fountain. In the warm weather meals were taken in that courtyard. When a famous and distinguished teacher was sitting at such a meal, people crowded into the courtyard to listen to his conversation and his table-talk, eager to miss no pearl of wisdom that might fall from his lips. It was at such a meal that Jesus was reclining. Into the courtyard there came a woman who loved Jesus for all that he had done for her soul. She had seen the bitterness and the hatred and the hostility in the eyes of his enemies every time they looked at him; she knew that they were venomously plotting to destroy him; and her one desire was to seize this opportunity to demonstrate her love.

Women in Palestine often carried little phials of highly concentrated very precious perfume, worn on a chain around their necks. These phials could cost as much as £40. The perfume perfumed the whole body, and it was so concentrated and so precious that it was meant to be used one little drop at a time. The woman came as a spectator and a listener at this meal. She did the only thing she could do to show the devotion of her heart; she would give to Jesus the only precious thing which she possessed. She poured, not a single drop, but the whole of her precious phial of perfume on his head, and then broke it. Maybe she broke it because of an eastern custom. In the East, when a very famous and distinguished man came to a meal, after the meal often the goblet from which he had drunk was broken into fragments, so that never again might it be touched by lesser lips.

The reaction of the disciples was shocked astonishment at what they regarded as this fantastic waste. The phial could have been sold for three hundred pence and the proceeds given to the poor (Mark 14.5). The penny in question was a *denarius*, which was worth about ninepence, which in Palestine was a day's wages for a working man. Here was almost a year's wages poured out in waste. At the feeding of the five thousand Philip said that two hundred *denarii* would hardly be enough to feed a crowd like that (John 6.7). The perfume could have been sold for enough to buy a meal for more than five thousand hungry people—and it had been emptied out on Jesus' head.

In answer to the words and thoughts of the disciples Jesus said three things. First, he said that, if a man wished to help the poor, opportunities would never be lacking, for did not the Scriptures say: 'The poor will never cease out of the land'? (Deut. 15.11). Second, he said that the woman had done this against the day of his burial. In Palestine the bodies of the beloved dead were first bathed, and then anointed with perfume, and then the flask which had contained the perfume was broken, and the fragments of it were laid in the tomb with the body. The woman had rendered to him the very service which people rendered to the bodies of those whom they had loved. Third, he said that the story of this lovely deed would go out into all the world, and, so long as the gospel story was told, men would never allow the memory of it to die.

This story tells us a great deal about the love which delights the heart of Jesus.

(i)   There is a certain extravagance in love. The alabaster phial of perfume was meant to be used drop by drop; it was meant to last for years, perhaps even for a life-time; but in a moment of utter devotion the woman poured it on the head of Jesus. Love does not stop nicely to calculate the less or more; love does not stop to work out how little it can respectably give. With a kind of divine extravagance love gives everything it has, and never counts the cost. Calculation is never any part of love.

(ii)   Love knows well that there are certain moments in life which come and which do not return. There were endless and limitless opportunities to help the poor, but, if that woman had not seized that moment to make known her love to Jesus, the opportunity would never have come again. There are moments in life which do not come a second time. Impulses to devotion, impulses to reformation, impulses to decision enter the heart, and, if they are not acted on at once, they may never return. Love is ever ready to seize the moment to declare itself.

(iii)   Love puts into the world a fragrance which time

cannot obliterate. To this day the story of that woman's devotion moves the heart. A lovely deed is not only a thing of the moment; it leaves something in the world which time cannot take away. Love adds a permanent legacy of loveliness to life.

This story has light to shed on the mind of Jesus.

(i)   Once again it tells us of his consciousness and his claim. In the Old Testament three kinds of people were anointed. *Priests* were anointed. The law runs: 'You shall take the anointing oil, and pour it on his[1] head and anoint him' (Ex. 29.7). *Prophets* were anointed. God's command to Elijah was to anoint Elisha his successor (I Kings 19.16). The prophet whom we call Third Isaiah speaks of himself as having been anointed to preach the good tidings (Isa. 61.1). *Kings* were anointed. It is God's command to Samuel to anoint Saul as king of the people (I Sam. 9.16), and later to anoint David (I Sam. 16.12f.). It was God's command to Elijah to anoint Hazael to be king of Syria (I Kings 19.15f.). Anointing was proper to the priest, the prophet and the king; and by accepting the action of this woman Jesus implicitly claimed to be the *Prophet* who brought to men the word of God, the *Priest* who built for men the bridge to God, the *King* who claimed from men a throne within their hearts. Even with the shadows closing around him, even amidst the misunderstanding of those closest to him, Jesus never lost the consciousness of his divine destiny.

(ii)   Once again we see Jesus perfectly aware of the death and the Cross which lay ahead of him. Anointing was given not only to the living but also to the dead. In the East the bodies of the dead were anointed and embalmed in perfumes and in sweet-smelling spices. It was that very office, as Jesus said, that the woman had performed for him. Humanly speaking, Jesus need never have gone back from Bethany into Jerusalem; he need never have left the circle of his

[1]   The priest's.

friends to enter the circle of his enemies. Humanly speaking, the way back was still perfectly possible, and the door of escape was still wide open. But Jesus went out knowing that the only arms which would welcome him in Jerusalem were the arms of the Cross.

(iii)   Once again we see Jesus confident of his ultimate vindication. It did not occur to him that his work would be obliterated; already he heard the story of the gospel echoing down the corridors of time. He envisaged a day when nothing less than the whole world would know of the lovely thing which this woman had done (Mark 14.9). He knew that men could crucify him, but he also knew that men were powerless to eliminate him from history. He who was on his way to the Cross looked forward to a day when all men would know his name.

5

THE BETRAYAL OF LOVE

IT is one of the tragic ironies of the Gospel narrative that, on the very day on which the woman in Bethany poured out upon Jesus the splendour of her love, Judas Iscariot took steps to arrange his betrayal to the leaders of the Jews (Matt. 26.14-16; Mark 14.10; Luke 22.3-6).

The mind of Judas must always be one of the great enigmas of history. The first three Gospels give us strangely little material about him, for they never so much as mention him between his call by Jesus at the beginning and his betrayal of Jesus at the end. Any information which we do possess comes from the Fourth Gospel, which was the last Gospel to be written, and which naturally tends to darken the picture of the traitor. Let us try, in so far as we can, to reconstruct the mind and the motives of Judas, using the material which the Fourth Gospel supplies.

(i) Judas was *the man whom Jesus called*. From the beginning he was one of the chosen twelve (Matt. 10.4; Mark 3.19; Luke 6.16). That basic fact tells us that Judas might have become great in the service of Jesus—but something went wrong. A certain writer wrote a series of studies on the twelve apostles and entitled it *The Men whom Jesus made*, but when he came to the study of Judas he headed it *The Man whom Jesus could not make*. Jesus never used men as a tradesman uses a tool; Jesus used men as a leader uses his willing followers. If Jesus was to use a man, that man had to consent to be used. Judas was the man whom

Jesus called, and the man who refused to be used in Jesus' way.

(ii) Judas was *the man whom Jesus warned*. John tells us of the feeding of the five thousand, and of the consequent movement to make Jesus king, a move which Jesus completely rejected. From that time many were disappointed in him and left him. Jesus thereupon asked his own chosen men if they too were going to leave him, and Peter immediately affirmed his loyalty and the loyalty of his fellow-apostles. Then Jesus said: 'Did not I choose you, the twelve—and one of you is a devil?' (John 6.70). It is quite certain that the rest of the apostles had no suspicion of what was going on in Judas' mind. If they had had any such suspicion, they would have dealt with Judas, even with violence. But Jesus knew, and he was telling Judas to stop in time. Judas was the man whom Jesus warned.

(iii) Judas was *the man to whom Jesus appealed*. There is no doubt that Judas held a leading place in the apostolic company. Jesus appointed Judas their treasurer (John 12.6). When Judas left the Upper Room before the last meal was ended, the disciples were not alarmed, for they thought that he had gone out to deal with the practical arrangements which Passover time necessitated (John 13.29). Often the best way to strengthen a waverer is to give him some special task to do, and often the best way to secure a man's loyalty is to show him that he is trusted. And Jesus tried that way with Judas.

Still clearer is the appeal of Jesus at the last meal together. From the story of that meal it is clear that Judas was in special honour. It was to him that Jesus handed the morsel of food called the sop, for it was thus that a host treated his most favoured guest (John 13.26; Matt. 26.23). The whole story makes it evident that Jesus could speak privately to Judas without the others hearing. Judas must, therefore, have been next to Jesus. In the East guests did not sit at table; the table was a low block and they reclined on couches, leaning on the left elbow, with the right hand free to use, and the feet stretched out behind. The couches usually held three. The place of honour was the place on the right of the host, for whoever was there reclined literally with his head on the breast of the host. That was the place occupied by the beloved disciple, who was most probably John (John 13.23). If Jesus was able to carry on a private conversation with Judas, Judas must have been on Jesus' left, and must have been the third person on the topmost couch. As John's head was on Jesus' breast, so Jesus' head must have been on Judas' breast. It is as if Jesus had deliberately bidden Judas to come and sit beside him that he might make to him a last appeal to halt in his dreadful undertaking. It may be that it was that seating arrangement, that special honour paid to Judas, which roused the strife and argument about precedence about which Luke tells (Luke 22.24-27).

The degeneration of Judas was no sudden affair; it was a long process; and all through it Jesus was making appeal after appeal to Judas in the hope of saving him from his self-chosen way of tragic disaster.

Neither warning nor appeal restrained Judas from his chosen way. The problem, however, was how to arrest Jesus without a riot; the one thing which Rome would never allow was civil disorder; and the Jewish authorities were puzzled to find some way to arrest Jesus without provoking any trouble. It was that problem which Judas was able to solve for them (Matt. 26.14-16; Mark 14.10f.; Luke 22.3-6). Ground was so limited in Jerusalem, the city built on the top of the hill, that there were no private gardens attached to the houses. The well-to-do had their private gardens on the slopes of the Mount of Olives outside the city. Some nameless friend had given Jesus the right to use his garden, and in the evening it was Jesus' custom, when he was in

Jerusalem, to retire to that garden for quiet and for prayer. Judas knew this, and it was thither that he proposed to lead the emissaries of the Jews so that the arrest could be carried out without disturbance. And in return for his information they gave him thirty silver pieces, thirty *staters*, the price of a slave, a little less than five pounds (Matt. 26.15).

By this time Judas was completely in the confidence of the authorities, and, when the time came, they gave him a band of men and officers of the Temple police to carry out the arrest. Judas was clearly the commander of the whole engagement. It would be a night of full moon, for it was at the full moon that the Passover took place. There would be light enough to see what must be done; but lest in the milling crowd there might be any mistake, Judas gave them a sign; he would identify Jesus with a kiss (Matt. 26.47-50; Mark 14.43-45; Luke 22.47f.). There would be nothing strange in that, for this was the way in which a disciple always greeted his Rabbi.

So through the agency of Judas Jesus was arrested; and then something very strange happens. Judas for the time being vanishes from the scene. At the beginning of the arrest Judas is obviously the leader of the whole operation; at the end of it he is not even there; and there is no mention of him at the trial, when witnesses against Jesus are being sought. Even as quickly as that something must have happened to Judas.

And then the curtain comes down on tragedy. The New Testament has two accounts of the end of Judas. One says that he went to the priests, tried to give them the money back, and, when they refused it, flung it at their feet, and went out and hanged himself (Matt. 27.3-5). The other account says that he bought a field with the money and there in some dreadful accident was killed (Acts 1.18). No matter which story we accept, the end of the matter for Judas was a broken life and a broken heart.

Such are the external facts of Judas' life as we know them, but what were the facts to his mind? What were the motives which moved him to the greatest act of treachery in history, and which made his name an epitome of all that makes a traitor?

(i) Luke and John both come to the same grim conclusion. Luke writes: 'Then Satan entered into Judas' (Luke 22.3). John writes: 'The devil had already put it into the heart of Judas Iscariot to betray him' (John 13.2). Just as God is looking for hands to use to do his work, so the devil is looking for them too, and the devil found his instrument in Judas. But the fact remains that no man can be used without his own consent. Judas is the man who consented to be used by the devil and by the powers of evil, for Judas could have kept the devil out of his life, and could have shut his heart against the tempter.

(ii) There is an apocryphal book called *The Story of Joseph of Arimathaea*. It has, of course, no claims to be considered as authentic history, but it has an interesting story of Judas. Its story is that Judas was the son of the brother of Caiaphas the High Priest, and that he was persuaded by the Jewish leaders to become a member of Jesus' inner circle with the deliberate intention that he might be a spy and a secret agent. According to this story, Judas was never a loyal or real disciple of Jesus, but was always the enemy agent cunningly inserted into Jesus' inner circle in due time to become the means whereby Jesus could be destroyed. This would mean that from the beginning the one intention of Judas was to find a way to compass the death of Jesus. This much at least is true, that Judas was prepared to become the tool whereby the Jewish authorities found a means to unleash their envenomed hatred upon Jesus.

(iii) One of the features of the first three Gospels is the extraordinary restraint with which they deal with the story of Judas. One might have expected them to paint the picture

of Judas in terms of the blackest horror, but in fact they
deal with him in silence. But the Fourth Gospel takes things
a little further. In John's story of the anointing at Bethany
it is Judas who leads the protest against the waste of the
money which the sale of the ointment might have procured.
But John's stinging comment is that the complaint of Judas
was not due to any compassion and care for the poor, but
to the fact, as the Authorized Version has it, that he was a
thief and had the bag, and '*bare* what was put therein'
(John 12.6). The word for 'to bear' is *bastazein*. Collo-
quially it can be used to mean 'to pilfer', as the Revised
Standard Version shows. *Bastazein* is used in Greek as the
word 'to lift' is used in Scots; it can be used either in the
sense of 'to carry' or 'to pilfer', as in the word 'a shoplifter'.
So, then, Judas was a lover of money and a thief. The
simplest interpretation of Judas is that in his love for money
he betrayed Jesus for no other reason than to gain the
promised reward. It may be so, and yet somehow that
seems an inadequate motive for the crime of Judas.

(iv)   It is most likely that we may find the clue to the
mind of Judas in his name. The name *Iscariot* may well be
connected with the word *sicarius*. The *sicarii* were literally
'the dagger-bearers'. The *sicarii* were fanatical Jewish
nationalists. They believed intensely in the destiny of Israel;
they believed that Israel was intended by God to rule the
world; but they believed that God would not help Israel
until the men of Israel helped themselves. They were therefore pledged to a campaign of murder, assault, assassina-
tion, sudden death, directed against the Romans; and they
drew their name from the fact that, concealed beneath their
robes, they carried daggers with which they were prepared
to murder any Roman who gave them any opportunity to
do so. They were patriots fanatical almost to the extent of
insanity. Such was the flame of their nationalism that they
were prepared not only to murder their Roman masters,

but also to murder any Jew who would not take their way of violence or who could be suspected of the least collaboration with Rome. They hated any Jew who was lukewarm in what they held to be patriotism almost as much as they hated the Romans.

It is more than likely that Judas was such a man. If he was, two possibilities open out. First, he may have seen Jesus, with his gift of words and with miraculous powers in his hands, as the heaven-sent leader for whom the Jews were waiting, the one who could put himself at the head of the loyalists of Palestine and so sweep the Romans from the land, and begin the campaign which was to lead to world conquest and world power. And then, when bit by bit he began to see that Jesus refused to take that way, in his bitter disillusionment he may have betrayed Jesus into the hands of his enemies. It is the very kind of thing that a disappointed 'dagger-bearer' would have done. But there is something even more likely than that. It may well be that Judas saw in Jesus the leader for whom he and his fellow-fanatics were waiting. Then he began to see that, as he thought, Jesus was wavering in his purpose. Then he took steps to place Jesus in the power of his enemies, not with any intention of compassing his death, but with the intention of placing him in a position in which in his own self-defence he would be bound to act, and bound to launch the long-awaited campaign. It may well be that when Judas said to Jesus: 'Hail, master!' and kissed him that there was no intended treachery, but that Judas was saying: 'Now is your chance to act! Blast them with your power!'

It is this alone which explains Judas' sudden disappearance from the scene, and his reappearance as a haunted man to commit suicide. He had suddenly in one blinding, agonizing moment discovered that his plan had gone wrong, and that he had killed the one he loved—and it may be that in one searing moment of revelation in the eyes of

Jesus he had seen that the whole dream on which he had built his life was an error and a delusion.

Judas was the man who tried to make Jesus that which he wished him to be instead of submitting to Jesus, so that he himself might become what Jesus wished him to be.

One tremendous truth the events of this Wednesday in the last week of Jesus demonstrate. On this day the woman at Bethany anointed him in overflowing love; on this day Judas betrayed him either in hate or in expectation. There is no possibility of neutrality in regard to Jesus. A man either desires to enthrone him in his heart or to eliminate him from his life.

6

LOVE'S MEMORIAL

BY the Thursday of the last week of his life, time for Jesus was running very short. It was on the Thursday that he ate the last meal in the upper room with the twelve. Out of that meal there has come to the Christian Church that sacrament which is the central act of the Church's worship, and it is, therefore, of special importance to seek the mind of Jesus in it. It so happens that the story of this last meal is beset by problems which are by no means easy of solution, and which yet must at least be faced, if we are to attempt to understand the mind of Jesus.

We may begin by noting one simple fact. For the Jew in the time of Jesus the day ended at sunset, not at midnight. This to our way of thinking has one curious consequence. To the Jew the new day began at 6 p.m. In the case of the Passover, the Passover Feast began on Thursday; that was the first day of the feast of the unleavened bread, or the day of preparation. It was on the Thursday that the lambs which were later to be eaten at the Passover feast were sacrificially slain in the Temple from just before midday until mid-afternoon. The feast of the Passover was itself in the evening of what we would call Thursday, but of what to the Jews was actually the beginning of Friday, since it was after 6 p.m. By our reckoning the preparation for the Passover, the first day of the feast of unleavened bread and the Passover all fall on Thursday; but to the Jew the first two fell on Thursday, and the third on Friday, because Thursday ended and Friday began at 6 p.m.

We must next face the problem that the first three Gospels and the Fourth Gospel regard the last meal of Jesus and the twelve as different things. There is no real doubt that the first three Gospels all regard the Last Supper as a Passover meal. They note that two days after the events at Bethany the Passover fell to be celebrated (Matt 26.2; Mark 14.1; Luke 22.1). Matthew and Mark say that on the first day of the feast of unleavened bread, that is, on the Thursday, Jesus despatched his disciples to Jerusalem to make the necessary preparations (Matt. 26.17; Mark 14.12). It was on that first day that the Passover was killed; that is to say, on that day the Passover lamb was sacrificially slain in the Temple (Mark 14.12; Luke 22.7). Jesus had sent them forward to find the room where he was to eat the Passover, and in accordance with his instructions they made ready the Passover (Matt. 26.19; Mark 14.16; Luke 22.13). When evening came, Jesus sat down with the twelve, and there is no doubt that we are meant to understand that it was the Passover feast at which they sat down together (Matt. 26.20; Mark 14.17; Luke 22.14). The first three Gospels distinctly set the Last Supper in the context of the Passover meal.

On the other hand the Fourth Gospel is just as definite that the crucifixion of Jesus took place *before* the Passover. John's account of that last meal together begins with the direct statement that it took place before the feast of the Passover (John 13.1). John tells us that the Jewish authorities would not enter Pilate's judgment hall, lest they be rendered unclean and so be unable to eat the Passover (John 18.28), and he thereby makes it quite clear that he conceived of the trial of Jesus as taking place before the Passover feast. John gives the day and time of the crucifixion, saying that it took place on the day of the preparation of the Passover at the sixth hour, that is, at twelve noon (John 19.14).

It is on the whole the aim of the writers of the first three Gospels to narrate the facts of the life of Jesus as they knew them; but it is the aim of the writer of the Fourth Gospel to penetrate beyond the immediate fact to the eternal truth of which the immediate fact is a symbol. When we remember that, it is of the greatest importance to note that, as John tells the story, *Jesus was crucified at exactly the same time as the Passover lambs were being sacrificially slain in the Temple.* There can be little doubt that John so tells the story in order to show that Jesus is the Passover lamb of God, whose shed blood brought deliverance to his people.

It is on the whole more likely that in the literal sense the first three Gospels are right, and that John has rearranged the facts to underline the fact that Jesus is the Passover lamb.

One further difficulty must be faced. The Passover lamb was central to the whole Passover feast, and yet in the narrative of the Gospels the lamb does not itself appear, except indirectly in the references to killing the Passover, that is, to sacrificing the Passover lamb and its blood on the afternoon of Thursday, and in the statement that the disciples sent on in advance made ready the Passover (Mark 14.12,16; Luke 22.7,13). But at the feast itself the Gospels do not mention the lamb. If this is felt as a real difficulty, then it is a possible explanation that what the Gospels tell is the story of the Passover Kiddush. *Kiddush* means a 'hallowing', a 'sanctifying', a 'setting apart'. All the great festivals, and in particular the Sabbath, were preceded by a *kiddush*, a hallowing. In the home a table was prepared, and thereon there was placed a cup, a jug of wine, and two loaves of bread. The wine was blessed and poured out; the bread was broken and shared out, the father of the family being the leader of the ceremony. This action was an introduction to the Sabbath, and to all the great festivals. It may be that the part of the Last Supper which is narrated to us is, in fact, not the Passover meal itself but rather the *kiddush* which preceded it. That would explain the absence of all reference to the lamb.

Now we must turn to the narratives to try to see through them the mind of Jesus himself.

The first thing which strikes us in the whole tenor of the narrative is that for Jesus this was no improvization. From beginning to end he gives the impression of having long ago prepared this, and of being in complete control. He knew precisely where and to whom he was sending on the disciples ahead to make their preparations (Matt. 26.17-19; Mark 14.12-16; Luke 22.7-13). They will find a house with a large upper room. If houses in Palestine had two rooms, the second room was the upper room. The houses were like a large box with a smaller box on top. The smaller box on top was the upper room, and was reached by an outside stair. It was used for storage and as a guest room; but in particular it was used as a place of prayer and as a place where a Rabbi met with his students and disciples to commune with them.

Jesus had already arranged with a nameless friend that such an upper room should be available for him and his disciples that they might keep the Passover. He had even arranged a signal so that his friend might be immediately recognizable. The disciples were to look for a man carrying a water-pot (Mark 14.13; Luke 22.10). Such a man would stand out unmistakably in the crowd. To carry a water-pot on the shoulder was woman's work, something which a man would never do. A man with a water-pot on his shoulder would be as prominent as a man in this country using, let us say, a lady's umbrella on a rainy day. Jesus had left nothing to chance, which shows how important he took this occasion to be.

The disciples went into the city; they found things as Jesus had said; and they made all the necessary preparations for the Passover (Matt. 26.19; Mark 14.16; Luke 22.13). The things necessary for the Passover were as follows. There was the lamb, which had to be killed in the Temple courts, and the blood of which, being the life, had to be poured out as an offering to God. There was the unleavened bread, to remind the Jews of the bread they had hastily baked without leaven, and had hastily eaten, on the night on which they had escaped from Egypt. There was a bowl of salt water, which stood for the salt tears which they had shed in Egypt, when they were slaves, and for the waters of the Red Sea through which they had escaped. There was the dish of bitter herbs—horse-radish, chicory, endive, horehound—to remind them of the bitterness of slavery. There was the *charosheth*, the paste of apples, nuts and pomegranates, to remind them of the clay with which they had made bricks in Egypt, with sticks of cinnamon running through it, to remind them of the straw which they had used. There was the wine, of which everyone who sat at the Passover must drink the four cups. It must be remembered that the Passover feast was a real meal; the minimum number which constituted a Passover company was ten; but every scrap of the food had to be eaten, and nothing must be left. So all things were prepared, and in the evening Jesus came with the twelve to eat the feast.

As we read the story, the atmosphere is the atmosphere of impending disaster; and in particular there were three moments instinct with tragedy. There was a strife among the disciples about which of them should be greatest (Luke 22.24-30). Even in the shadow of the Cross personal ambitions and thoughts of personal prestige and envies and jealousies invaded the circle. There was the moment when Jesus declared his knowledge of the traitor in the midst (Matt. 26.21-24; Mark 14.18-21; Luke 22.21-23). It is only Matthew and John who actually identify the traitor as Judas Iscariot (Matt. 26.25; John 13.26-30), and it is quite certain that the other disciples cannot have known the evil purposes of Judas, or they would have attacked him there and then. John speaks of Jesus handing to Judas the morsel, or the sop. About halfway through the feast some of the bitter herbs were placed between two pieces of unleavened bread, dipped in the paste of the *charosheth*, and so eaten, and that was the morsel or sop. So at the Last Supper treachery was there. There was the moment when Jesus foretold the coming denial of which Peter would be so tragically guilty. According to Matthew and Mark it was on the way to Gethsemane (Matt. 26.30-35; Mark 14.26-31) that Jesus gave Peter his warning; but according to Luke it was in the upper room itself (Luke 22.31-34). Peter was sure that not even the threat of death would make him disloyal, but Jesus warned him that his loyalty would not stand the test. So at the Last Supper personal ambition with its attendant bitterness and strife, treachery, disloyalty were all present to drive their nails through the heart of Jesus even before the Cross.

We must now try to see what the mind of Jesus was in that last meal together; and here we have another problem. The words which Jesus spoke are by no means certain. The form of the words which we commonly use in our own celebration and observance of the sacrament is the form which is found, not in the Gospels, but in Paul's First Letter to Corinth. In that form Jesus gives thanks and breaks the bread and says: 'This is my body which is for you. Do this in remembrance of me.' He then takes the cup after the meal, and says: 'This cup is the new covenant in my blood. Do this, as often as you drink it, in remembrance of me' (I Cor. 11.23-26). It may be noted that I Corinthians was in fact written earlier than any of the three Gospels, and that this is in fact the first *written* account of the Last Supper. In Matthew and Mark the best texts omit the word 'new' before the word 'covenant'. Both Matthew and Mark have: 'This is my blood of the covenant which is poured out for many,' to which Matthew alone adds, 'for the forgiveness of sins' (Matt. 26.28; Mark 14.24). In the best text of Luke, Luke 22.19 reads simply: 'And he took bread, and when he had given thanks he broke it and gave it to them, saying, This is my body.' That is to say, the words, 'which is given for you,' and the words, 'This do in remembrance of me,' are not in the best texts of Luke. Further, the best texts of Luke omit Luke 22.20 altogether: 'Likewise the cup after supper, saying: This cup which is poured for you is the new covenant in my blood.' It can, therefore, be seen that the great difference between the account of the Last Supper in the Gospels, if the best text be followed, and the account in I Corinthians is that in the Gospels the idea of the *new* covenant is not so strongly stressed, and the injunction to repeat the actions of the bread and wine is not there at all. In seeking to interpret these words, and in seeking to read the mind of Jesus in them, we must, therefore, be careful to confine ourselves to those ideas and conceptions which are basic to both accounts. What, then, are those ideas?

(i) At the background of the whole meal there lies *the Passover*. This remains true whether or not the meal itself was actually a Passover feast or not. The whole action takes place in the context of the Passover, and with the Passover uppermost in the minds of those who partook of it. Now the basic idea of the Passover is emancipation, deliverance from the bondage and the slavery of Egypt, and safety through the blood of the Passover lamb, smeared on the doorpost of the houses of the children of Israel, when the angel of death slew the firstborn in the land of Egypt (Ex. 12). Jesus is, therefore, setting himself before men in terms of emancipation, liberation, redemption, freedom—and that liberation can only be from sin. Further, he is setting himself before men as the sacrifice for men, for it was the sacrificial blood of the slain lamb which preserved the people in the day of the destruction wrought by the wrath of God. First, then, there is the idea of redemption through sacrifice.

(ii) The second idea which runs through the whole action is the idea of *the covenant*. It does not matter whether

the word *new* is inserted or not, the basic idea will remain
the same. The essence of a covenant is the establishment of
a new relationship between God and man on the initiative
of God. But in any event there is an essential difference
between the old covenant and the covenant which Jesus
claimed to establish. The old covenant was founded and
based on, and was dependent on, obedience to the law.
Failure to obey the law and to keep the law meant the end
of the relationship involved in the covenant (Ex. 24.1-8).
But the covenant of which Jesus speaks is established and
maintained by his blood, by his life and his death. That is to
say, he is claiming that through him, and through his life and
his death, a new relationship between God and man has
become possible.

These two ideas become one when we remember that the
whole sacrificial system of the Jews had as its one aim and
object the restoration of the relationship between God and
man which breaches of the law had interrupted. Jesus, therefore, was saying that the sacrifice of his life and his death
made possible for ever and for ever a relationship between
sinful man and holy God, a relationship apart altogether
from law, and therefore a relationship of love.

What, then, must this sacrament of the Lord's Supper be
to us? It is basic to remember that Jesus was here again
using the method of symbolic action which the prophets had
so often used, as he did when he came riding into Jerusalem.
He was putting a message into dramatic action, the effect of
which was meant to be more vivid than any words. If that be
so, it is quite certain that in the action of the bread and wine
Jesus was seeking to imprint indelibly upon the minds of his
men that which he was and that which he had come to do.
The Lord's Supper is, then, first and foremost a means of
memory. It is the memorial of Jesus. It is meant to act as a
stabbing awake of the memory which has become forgetful

or lethargic. The human mind forgets; time, as the Greeks said, wipes all things out, as if the mind were a slate and time an erasing sponge; even the most poignant event loses its poignancy as the years go on; so Jesus offered men this action which in the beginning set forth his own claim and which for time to come was to remind them of his claim and of his sacrifice.

But it is necessary to go beyond that. The bare statement that the Lord's Supper is a memorial and a stimulus to memory carries its own inadequacy upon its face. A memory is necessarily a memory of someone or of something who or which is no longer here, but is gone from sight and from life. But Jesus is not the one who is gone; he is the risen Lord; he is the ever-present one in virtue of his risen life and his conquest of death. As it has been vividly put: 'No apostle ever *remembered* Jesus.' Jesus is not a memory to be called to mind; he is a presence to be met and a person to be experienced. Therefore, the Lord's Supper must be not only memory; it must be also confrontation. It is confrontation with the risen Lord. This is not even for one moment to say that the Christian cannot meet his Lord anywhere; but at the Lord's Supper everything is prepared to make that confrontation inevitable and deliberately to invite it. It is the compelling of the forgetful memory and the cold heart to become vividly aware of that presence which can otherwise be so easily unrealized and forgotten.

But confrontation must necessarily be to some purpose. Now Jesus in the meeting in the upper room with his disciples, as we have seen, presented himself to them in terms of emancipation, deliverance, redemption into a new relationship with God through the sacrificial love of his life and his death. Therefore, for us the Lord's Supper is not only confrontation; it must also be appropriation. In it we must realize the presence of Jesus Christ and we must appropriate the deliverance, the emancipation, the redemption he offers us, and so enter into the new relationship with God. The Lord's Supper is confrontation with the aim and purpose of the appropriation of the saving benefits of Jesus Christ.

It may be that we must still add something to this, and it may be that it is to this end that the tragic incidents of the strife of personal ambition, the tragedy of the traitor, and the heartbreak of disloyalty and denial are fitted into the story. The Lord's Supper must be realization. It must be the realization of the terrible, destructive power of sin, the realization that sin destroys personal relationships, leads a man to betray his Lord and to deny the one he loves, and in the end breaks upon a cross the loveliest of all lives. Therefore, there is a sense in which the Lord's Supper is not only the revelation of the love of God in Jesus Christ, but is also the revelation of the sin of man. The Lord's Supper ought to make him who participates in it realize his own sin, and then it ought to make him avail himself of the one way in which that sin can be conquered and overcome and finally defeated.

There remains one question to be asked. Where is all this to happen? In the narrative of the Gospels we have no word in regard to the continual repetition of the action of the bread and wine, and yet the very fact that that repetition is taken for granted in Paul's account of the Last Supper in I Corinthians shows that, even before the Gospels were written, the Church never doubted that the dramatic and symbolic action of the bread and wine was intended to be repeated. But *what* was intended to be repeated? 'This do in remembrance of me.' Does it mean that this dramatic action was to be re-enacted as each Passover came round, or as each *Kiddush* came week by week? Does it mean that some kind of symbolic action has to be repeated, which is in fact what has happened? The Church, at least in modern times, has made out of the Last Supper not a meal but the symbol of a meal. Can it be that at least in part we have been mistaken as to the intention of Jesus?

It remains a curious fact that in the Gospel narrative there is no definite instruction as to repetition, and from this there emerges a possibility of the greatest significance. We have before stressed the fact that the Passover meal was a real meal, and very far from the taking of a sip of wine and the eating of a fragment, a cube, or a wafer of bread. It remains a very definite possibility that Jesus did not intend to institute a symbolic meal, but that he meant that every time bread was broken and eaten, and every time wine was poured out and drunk—that is, at every meal in every house —he was to be remembered. He may well have meant that every meal was a sacrament, that it should be impossible for any Christian at any time to break bread without remembering him. It has been said that we are not fully Christian until Christ has become Lord not only of the communion table but also of the dinner table. It may well be that the symbolic meal became a necessity with the vast growth of the Christian Church and the vast numbers of the Christian fellowship, when great congregations began to be built up; but it remains a real possibility that in the upper room Jesus was not intending to institute a special meal but that he was hallowing and sanctifying every common meal so that every meal might become an experience of his presence.

However that may be, it is the mind of Jesus that in the sacrament of the Lord's Supper we should remember him, we should confront and experience him, we should appropriate his saving work, we should realize the awfulness of sin and the wonder of God's cure for sin; and it is his will that in the end we should become so mindful of him that every common meal should become a sacrament of memory and of experience.

7

THE POINT OF NO RETURN

IN every long aeroplane flight there comes the point which the pilot knows as the point of no return. From then on he cannot go back, and he must go on. From that moment he has passed the point when return is possible. Just so, it is true that in every human exploit and undertaking there come the point of no return, the moment when the way back ceases to be possible, and when there is nothing left but to go on. For Jesus that moment came in the Garden of Gethsemane.

The last meal together had ended, and it ended with a hymn of praise. 'When they had sung a hymn, they went out to the Mount of Olives' (Matt. 26.30; Mark 14.26). Part of the ritual of the Passover was the singing of the *Hallel*. The word *Hallel* means 'Praise God'; and the *Hallel* consisted of Pss. 113-118, which are all praising psalms. Two of these psalms were sung midway through the Passover feast, and four of them were sung near the end. Finally, just before the feast came to an end with the blessing, the *Great Hallel* was sung. This was Ps. 136, with its constantly recurring refrain: 'O give thanks to the Lord, for he is good, for his steadfast love endures for ever.' It was with a great cry of praise that Jesus went out to the agony of body, mind and spirit which lay ahead.

Gethsemane means 'the Oil Press'. Jerusalem was built on the strictly circumscribed area on the top of Mount Sion. Because of this there was no space for gardens, and the well-to-do had their gardens on the slopes of the Mount of Olives, which were reached by descending from Jerusalem into the ravine through which the Kidron flowed, and then climbing the slopes of the hill on the other side. Gethsemane must have been such a little enclosed garden on the slopes of the Mount of Olives, and some nameless friend must have given Jesus permission to use it during the Passover week. So out of the upper room into the garden Jesus went. The story of the garden is in Matt. 26.36-46; Mark 14.32-42; Luke 22.40-46, and from it certain things unmistakably emerge.

In the garden we see the *loneliness* of Jesus. He took with him Peter, James and John to share his vigil; but they were so physically exhausted and so emotionally drained that sleep overcame them. Jesus had to take his decision alone. And this is symbolic of all life, for there are certain things which are between a man and God, and which have to be settled in the awful loneliness of a man's own soul.

In the garden we see the *mental agony* of Jesus. There was the sheer physical side of the matter. No man wishes to die at thirty-three, least of all to die in the terrible agony of a cross, for the cross had a lingering agony such as no other form of execution had. There was the mental agony of the situation. Humanly speaking, Jesus was going to death with so little done and so much to do. His supporters were so few, so uncomprehending and ununderstanding, and so unreliable when danger threatened. His opponents were so solidly powerful, for the leaders of orthodox religion were unitedly against him. Humanly speaking, the mission of Jesus seemed to be drawing to its close in failure.

In the garden we see the *spiritual agony* of Jesus. It may be that some will find it impossible to accept the view which we have earlier expressed, but as we read the story of the garden we cannot but feel that the very essence of the matter is that Jesus was accepting that which he did not fully understand. He knew that the Cross was for him the will of God, but at the moment he could not see why it had to be the Cross. He knew that he must drink the cup, but he did not fully know why the cup must be. Unless Jesus knew this acceptance of that which he did not fully understand, he did not enter fully into the deeps of the human situation, for it is precisely this that being a man involves. But we must go further than this.

In the garden we see Jesus *accepting the will of God*; but what is all important is the way in which he accepted it. In Mark's version of the story there is something of infinite beauty and of infinite value. As Mark tells the story Jesus said: '*Abba*, Father, all things are possible to thee; remove this cup from me; yet not what I will, but what thou wilt' (Mark 14.36). The essence of that whole saying lies in the completely untranslatable word *Abba*. As Jeremias points out, Jesus' use of the word *Abba* to God is completely without parallel. That was an address which no one had ever used to God before. Why? Because in Palestine in the time of Jesus *Abba*, as *jaba* is today in Arabic, was the word used in the home circle by a very young child to his father. No English translation can be anything other than grotesque; Jesus in that dark and terrible hour spoke to God as a little child speaks to the father whom he trusts and loves.

Here is the essence of Gethsemane. The whole meaning and significance of the words, 'Thy will be done,' depend on the tone of the voice and the feeling of the heart with which they are spoken. They may be spoken in broken and abject surrender, as by one who is beaten to his knees by some superior and ineluctable force, and has given up the battle. They may be spoken in weary resignation, as by one who has come to see and to admit that further resistance is useless, and who dully and hopelessly gives in. They may be spoken in bitter resentment, as by one who has ceased to struggle but whose whole heart and being are rising up in rebellion against the situation in which he finds himself, as by one who has accepted the inevitable but who still shakes his fist in the face of fate. They may be spoken in utter love and trust, as by one who does not need to understand in order to submit, who knows that a father's hand will never cause his child a needless tear, who knows that he is not the plaything of circumstance or the victim of the blind tyranny of God, or the sport of blind chance and fate, but who is certain that he can take life and leave it in God's hand and be content. Jesus in Gethsemane is the great example of submission to the will of God, even when that will is a mystery, in the certainty that that will is love.

In Gethsemane Jesus passed the point of no return, and passed it in perfect trust in God.

No sooner had Jesus come to his great decision than the quiet of the garden was broken by the trample of feet, the clank of arms, and the shouting of men. The nervous fear of the Jewish authorities is clear in the size of the force which they sent to arrest Jesus, as if he had been a man of violence (Matt. 26.47,55; Mark 14.43,48; Luke 22.52).

So the drama unfolded itself. First, there was the traitor's kiss (Mark 14.44f.; Matt. 26.48f.; Luke 22.47f.). The tragedy is deepened by the fact that both Matthew and Mark use the Greek word *kataphilein*, which means not only 'to kiss', but 'to kiss tenderly', as a lover might. Then there came Peter's desperate rearguard action, in which he showed himself ready to sell his life dearly in defence of Jesus his Lord and friend (Mark 14.47; Matt. 26.51f.; Luke 22.49-51; John 18.10f.). And finally there came the arrest. In the arrest the action of Jesus makes certain things quite clear.

(i) It is clear that Jesus went voluntarily to death. It is his own saying that he could have called on legions of angels to defend him, had he so willed (Matt. 26.53). As John tells the story, those who came to arrest Jesus were themselves so terrified that Jesus actually had to urge them to do their work (John 18.4-9). No man took Jesus' life from him; willingly he laid it down. Jesus was not the victim of God; he was the servant of God.

(ii) In all this Jesus saw the fulfilment of Scripture (Matt. 26.54; Mark 14.49). This was not an emergency in which affairs and events had got out of control; this was nothing less than an event to which all history had been pointing. Whatever things might look like, God was still in control, and God's redemptive purpose was still being worked out.

(iii) Luke has something which is basic and fundamental to the thought of the New Testament writers. Luke tells us that Jesus said: 'This is your hour, and the power of darkness' (Luke 22.53). All through the New Testament there runs the tremendous paradox of the Cross. The Cross was somehow at one and the same time part of the purpose, the design, the plan of God, and an awful and a dreadful crime at the hands of men. Nowhere does this come out with such absolute clarity as in Peter's sermon at Pentecost. There Peter says: 'This Jesus, being delivered up according to the definite plan and foreknowledge of God, you crucified and killed by the hands of lawless men' (Acts 2.23). Here in this death of Jesus, in the whole drama of the action of the last days, we see fully displayed the sin of man and the love of God.

(iv) As the arrest works itself out, as it becomes clear that Jesus would lift no hand to defend himself, there came the tragic end, for in that moment all the disciples 'forsook him and fled' (Matt. 26.56; Mark 14.50). The end of the road was something which Jesus had to walk alone. There was a part of his work in which no man could help him, and which he had to face in all the loneliness of his soul—until in the end he felt himself forsaken, not only by men, but even by God.

One thing remains. Even when we have set the tragedy of

the garden and the arrest at its blackest, its bitterest and its starkest, one indelible impression remains; and that is that in it and through it Jesus was always completely in control. He was never the helpless victim; he was always master of circumstance. Somehow even here there lie beneath the surface the first indications of the final triumph. The story never reads like the arrest of a criminal, unwillingly haled to judgment and to death; the story always reads like the willing sacrifice of one who of his own free will laid down his life for his friends.

8

THE TRIAL OF JESUS

IF we would see what the trial of Jesus in fact was, we must begin by seeing what in justice it ought to have been. Here we are in a difficulty. Capital trials of national and supreme religious importance were carried out by the Great Sanhedrin. In the *Mishnah* we have the tractate on the Sanhedrin, and we have the *Tosefta*, or commentary or expansion of it. These set out the jurisdiction, the powers, and the procedure of the Sanhedrin. But it is sometimes argued that the account of the Sanhedrin and its procedure given in the *Mishnah* is highly idealized, and that it is not to be taken as an account of actual practice. It certainly is the fact that the Sanhedrin probably never functioned in the ideal terms of the *Mishnah*. Nevertheless it is still true that the account of the procedure of the Sanhedrin in the *Mishnah* does give us two things. It does give us the broad lines on which the Sanhedrin acted, and it quite certainly gives us the *ideal* of justice, at which the Sanhedrin at least should have aimed in its procedure and in its practice. It is by no means illegitimate to set down the *Mishnah's* account of the Sanhedrin, and to examine the trial of Jesus in the light of it, for, whatever be true of the actual procedure of the trial, very certainly in it the Jewish authorities flouted every ideal of Jewish justice.

The Sanhedrin was the supreme court of the Jews. It was composed of seventy members, for that was the number of elders whom Moses appointed to aid him in his task (Num.

11.16), and its total membership was seventy-one, because it was presided over by the High Priest. In it there were scribes and Pharisees, priests and Sadducees, and elders of the people. It had jurisdiction over every Jew, and in the days of its independence it could impose the death penalty either by stoning, burning, beheading, or strangulation.

The great characteristic of the Sanhedrin was that everything was deliberately arranged and ordered to conserve the interests of the man on trial. The rabbinic aim was to exercise 'mercy in judgment'. It was said that the Sanhedrin was only exercising its true function when it acted as 'a counsel for the defence'. Even if there seemed to be no extenuating circumstances, it was the duty of the judges deliberately to try to find some. So much so was this the case that in the tractate *Makkoth* (1.10) it is laid down that 'the Sanhedrin which condemns to death one man in seven years is accounted murderous', and Rabbi Eleazar ben Azaria would have said, not one man in seven years, but one man in seventy years. Two famous rabbis who lived in the days when the Sanhedrin had ceased to possess the power of carrying out the death penalty declared that, if they had lived in the days when the Sanhedrin possessed that power, no one would ever have been condemned to death. It is almost true to say that ideally the Sanhedrin was organized to defend the man on trial.

Even the production and the examination of witnesses were governed by regulations which were meant to protect the interests of the accused. It was a fundamental principle of Jewish law that the evidence of two witnesses at least was always necessary for condemnation (Deut. 17.6). Salvador, the great Spanish Jewish doctor, laid down the four rules which ought to govern criminal procedure—strictness in the accusation, publicity in the discussion, full freedom granted to the accused, assurance against all dangers or errors in testimony. The procedure of the Sanhedrin was designed to satisfy these demands. The two witnesses were examined separately. The *Mishnah* lays it down that there are seven basic questions which a witness ought to be asked about any event about which he is giving evidence. In what Sabbatic period did it happen? In what year? In what month? On what date of the month? On what day (of the week)? At what hour? Where? Before anything could be done the evidence of the witnesses must exactly agree. One curious feature of legal procedure in the Sanhedrin was that the man involved was held to be absolutely innocent, and, indeed, not even on trial, until the evidence of the witnesses had been stated and confirmed. The argument about the case could only begin when the testimony of the witnesses was given and confirmed. That is the point of the conversation between Jesus and Annas in John 18.19-21. Jesus in that incident was reminding Annas that he had no right to ask him anything until the evidence of witnesses had been taken and found to agree.

Certain people were debarred by law from giving evidence —dice-players, pigeon-fliers, those who traded with the Sabbatic growth (Lev. 25.1ff.), usurers, robbers, herdsmen, extortioners, those who were suspect concerning property— that is to say, any whose honesty was under suspicion. Close relations could not give evidence. A man's friend and his enemy were alike disqualified. His friend was defined as his groomsman, and his enemy defined as 'a man who from hostility had not spoken to his neighbour for three days'.

Witnesses were compelled to appear, not only at the beginning of a trial, but also at the end, and in the case of stoning were under obligation to be the first to cast the stone at the accused, if he was found guilty. In capital cases witnesses were reminded of Gen. 4.10, in which God says to Cain: 'Your brother's blood is now crying to me from the ground.' It was pointed out that in the Hebrew the word *blood* is in the plural and is really *bloods*; and it was argued that the word meant not only the man himself, but also his as yet unborn posterity. So a witness was warned that, if by false witness he compassed the execution of the man on trial, he was no better than the murderer of that man and of his posterity in the sight of God.

The court itself could meet officially only in the Hall of Hewn Stone in the precincts of the Temple. Its members sat in a semi-circle so that each could see, and be seen, by all the others. In front there were two clerks of the court, one to take down the evidence for the prosecution, and one to take down the evidence for the defence. The disciples of the rabbis sat in three rows facing the court, each of them having his own seat. Should a new judge be needed, one from the front row of the disciples joined the court; the rows of the disciples then closed up, and one from the audience was chosen to fill the vacant place. The *Tosefta* gives the curious fact that there were four cubits—that is six feet—between each of the disciples, in order no doubt to put an end to whispered and private discussion. It is also laid down that capital cases could only be tried by judges who were priests, Levites, and Israelites eligible for marriage into priestly families, that is, by those whose lineage was absolutely pure. The *Tosefta* adds the fact that those who had no children and eunuchs could not act as judges in capital cases, which is another way of saying that only married men could act as judges in such cases.

In capital cases there must never be fewer than twenty-three judges. The case always began with the arguments for the acquittal of the prisoner. In non-capital cases a judge could alter either his pleading or his verdict in either direction; but in capital cases one who had pleaded against the prisoner could plead for him, but one who had pleaded for the prisoner could not in any circumstances plead against him, and similarly one who had voted for the condemnation of the prisoner could change his mind and vote for the acquittal of the prisoner, but one who had voted for the acquittal could not change sides and vote for condemnation. In capital cases verdicts had to be given individually, beginning with the youngest member of the court and going on to the eldest. Acquittal required a majority of only one; condemnation required a majority of at least two. Non-capital cases could be tried and ended on the same day; but in capital cases a verdict of acquittal could be given on the same day, and the prisoner immediately released, but a verdict of condemnation could not be finally pronounced until the following day, so that after a night's thought and meditation and prayer there might still be the opportunity to alter the verdict and to set the prisoner free. That was one of the reasons why a capital trial could never take place on the day before the Sabbath or the day before a great festival, for on such days the Sanhedrin could not meet. That is also the reason why capital trials could not be held at night.

One thing further must be noted. It was illegal to put to a prisoner a question by answering which he might condemn himself, and no prisoner could be found guilty on the basis of his own answers. The evidence on which he was found guilty must be the evidence of others who were independent witnesses. Maimonides says: 'Our law condemns no one to death on his own confession.' Bartenora says: 'It is a fundamental principle with us that no one can harm himself by what he says under trial.' To put questions to the accused by answering which he might incriminate himself, and then to condemn him on the strength of his own answers, was a complete reversal of the Jewish ideas of justice.

It is against all this background that we must visualize the trial of Jesus. It is not claimed that all these regulations were ever wholly carried out in practice by the Sanhedrin, although quite certainly many of them were, but it cannot be disputed that these regulations show the ideal at which the practice and procedure of the Sanhedrin aimed.

When we put together the material in the four Gospels we find that within the twelve hours of the night before his crucifixion Jesus underwent a trial that fell into six parts, and that he must have gone through an experience calculated to exhaust a man's body, to benumb his mind, to drain his emotions, and to break his spirit, and that yet in fact he emerged from this terrible ordeal unbroken and unbowed.

(i) First Jesus was brought *before Annas* immediately after his arrest (John 18.13,14). In the days of the independence of the Jews the office of High Priest had been for life; but in the days of Israel's servitude the office of High Priest had become a matter of personal intrigue and political manipulation, so that Tiberius could say that High Priests came and went 'like flies on a sore'. At this time Annas was not High Priest, although some years before he had held office; but since four of his sons had been, or were to be, High Priests, and since Caiaphas was his son-in-law, Annas was very much the power behind the throne. If the stalls in the Temple which Jesus had overturned really were the property of Annas and his family, no doubt Annas used his position to arrange that Jesus should be brought to him first, that he might gloat over the downfall of the presumptuous Galilaean.

(ii) Next, during the night, Jesus was taken to *the house of Caiaphas*, the actual High Priest, and examined there (Matt. 26.57-68; Mark 14.53-65; Luke 22.54,63-65; John 18.19-24). This must have been, not an official meeting of the Sanhedrin, but a kind of preliminary examination, held in order to examine Jesus with a view to formulating a definite charge on which to bring him before the Sanhedrin proper.

(iii) Next, very early in the morning *the Sanhedrin* proper met in order to carry out the official trial and to arrive at the official condemnation (Matt. 27.1f.; Mark 15.1;

Luke 22.66-71). In the days of Jewish independence this would have been the end of the matter, but at this time the Jews were under Roman rule; and the *Talmud* tells us that 'forty years before the destruction of the Temple the judgment of capital causes was taken away from Israel'. This necessitated the next step in the trial.

(iv)   There was the trial *before Pilate*, the Roman procurator (Matt. 27.2-26; Mark 15.2-15; Luke 23.1-5,13-25). This was the Roman stage of the trial.

(v)   There was the trial *before Herod* (Luke 23.6-12). Galilee was not within Pilate's jurisdiction; it was under Herod Antipas, who held his power and enjoyed the courtesy title of king by grace and favour of the Romans. Since Jesus was a Galilaean, Pilate sent him to Herod in order to avoid the responsibility of himself giving a verdict; but Herod sent Jesus back to Pilate with no verdict.

(vi)   Lastly there was the completion of the trial *before Pilate*, and the final condemnation.

It is quite true that, when we try to put the narratives of all the Gospels together, there is a certain amount of confusion. Only John tells of the examination before Annas. It seems clear that Matthew and Mark think of the examination of Jesus as happening during the night, while Luke makes it happen early in the morning (Luke 22.66). Matthew and Mark quite clearly thought that the meeting in the house of Caiaphas during the night was an actual meeting of the Sanhedrin (Matt. 26.59; Mark 14.55); and yet all three Gospels make it clear that there was a meeting of the Sanhedrin early in the morning (Matt. 27.1; Mark 15.1; Luke 22.66). But, whatever confusions there may be, and even if it is not possible to make an hour-to-hour time-table of the events of that night, there is no reasonable doubt as to the course the trial took, the treatment Jesus received, and the charges which in the end were levelled against him. On the whole the likeliest sequence of events is the arrest in the garden, the examination before Annas, the preliminary trial in the house of Caiaphas, all during the night of Thursday on our reckoning, but the beginning of Friday by Jewish reckoning; then came the official meeting of the Sanhedrin on the Friday morning and the trial before Pilate, with the despatch of Jesus to Herod as an interlude. Let us, then, look at the main events of the Jewish part of the trial.

The trial began with a search for witnesses on whose evidence Jesus could be charged. Many false witnesses were prepared to testify, but the story of no two agreed (Matt. 26.59f.; Mark 14.56). According to Mark, no two witnesses agreed to the end of the day (Mark 14.59); according to Matthew, at last two were found whose fabricated evidence did agree (Matt. 26.60f.). The evidence which in the end was produced claimed to prove that Jesus had said that he would destroy the Temple and that he would replace it within three days with a Temple not made with hands (Matt. 26.61; Mark 14.58). To this charge Jesus made no answer at all, meeting it with silence (Matt. 26.62f.; Mark 14.60f.). It may well be that this was a twisted version of something which Jesus did say, for the very same thing is referred to in John 2.19-22, and it was on that very charge that Stephen was later to be condemned (Acts 6.14). It may go back to one of two things. Either it may go back to a saying of Jesus about his own death and resurrection, as indeed John explains it (John 2.21), or, and this may well be more likely, it may go back to some statement of Jesus in which he said that the Temple would one day no longer be necessary for the worship of God, as, again according to John, he did say to the woman of Samaria (John 4.21). If that is so, the saying was not a threat against the Temple, but a condemnation of the exclusiveness of Temple worship. In any event, the Jews did not proceed upon that charge, thus tacitly admitting the utter worthlessness of the evidence of their own witnesses.

Then there came the real charge, and the events which led up to a charge of blasphemy. The High Priest asked Jesus the direct question, whether he claimed to be the Messiah (Matt. 26.63; Mark 14.61; Luke 22.67); and Jesus unequivocally replied that he was (Matt. 26.64; Mark 14.62; Luke 22.70). And then he went on: 'I tell you, hereafter you will see the Son of man seated at the right hand of Power, and coming on the clouds of heaven' (Matt. 26.64; Mark 14.62; Luke 22.69).

It is important to understand what Jesus was saying and claiming, for this is a much misunderstood text. Very often this saying of Jesus is taken as a prophecy of his coming again, although it is to be noted that Luke has it in a form where there is not even a suggestion of the coming again— 'But from now on the Son of man shall be seated at the right hand of the power of God' (Luke 22.69). Quite undoubtedly Jesus was quoting from Dan. 7.13f.:

'I saw in the night visions,
and behold,
there came with the clouds of heaven one like a son of man,
and he came to the Ancient of Days, and was presented
[before him.
And to him was given dominion and glory and kingdom,
that all peoples, nations and languages should serve him;
his dominion is an everlasting dominion, which shall not
[pass away,
and his kingdom one that shall not be destroyed.'

Now one thing is quite certain—the Daniel passage does not describe an arrival *on earth*; it describes a regal and triumphant arrival *in heaven*. What Jesus was prophesying was his own return to, and enthronement in, glory. He was saying: 'At this moment I may seem to be in your power.

At this moment you are gloatingly certain that you are going to eliminate me by having me nailed to a cross. This moment looks like your triumph and my defeat. But the day will come when you will see me again, and I shall be sitting in glory on the throne of God. At this moment you are the judges and I am the judged; the day will come in the heavenly places when I shall be the judge and when you will be on trial for your sins before me. At this moment you think that you are breaking me; the time will come when you will see me as the King of glory.' Here is the expression of the complete confidence of Jesus in his ultimate triumph.

Now, as the Jewish authorities saw it, they had their charge. This was blasphemy, treason against God; and Jesus must die.

If this preliminary trial of Jesus be set against the prescribed procedure of the Sanhedrin, in point after point it breaks the Sanhedrin's own regulations. The witnesses were false witnesses, and, even at that, if Mark is right, no two of them agreed. Jesus was from the beginning assumed to be guilty, even before the evidence of the witnesses was heard, when he should have been regarded as innocent and not even on trial until the evidence of his guilt was certain. He was twice subjected to physical violence (Luke 22.63; John 18.22). He was asked questions by answering which he was bound to incriminate himself, and he was in the end condemned on evidence which he himself supplied. The Sanhedrin met during the night and during the Passover, when it should not have met, and in the house of Caiaphas, whereas the only place in which it could lawfully meet was the Hall of Hewn Stone. The verdicts were not given in order, as the regulations laid down. It was in fact the case that a *unanimously* unfavourable verdict was illegal.[1] Some one had to take the accused's part. A night did not elapse

---

[1]   *Mishnah*, Sanhedrin 4.1.

between the first conviction and the final verdict. The whole spirit of Sanhedrin procedure was broken, for the court acted, not as counsel for the defence, but as counsel for the prosecution, and instead of conserving the rights of the prisoner it systematically destroyed them. Even if we concede that some, or even many, of these regulations were ideal rather than actual, the fact remains that the Jewish authorities were prepared to go to any lengths and to sink to any depths to compass the death of Jesus.

As for Jesus, three things stand out about him. There is his dignity, for all through the scene it is he who seems to be in control. There is his courage, for he gave his answer to the High Priest well knowing that it meant death, and well knowing that he could have temporized, or denied his destiny, and so saved his life. There is his complete confidence in his ultimate triumph, and in the glory beyond the Cross.

As we have seen, in the time of Jesus the Jews, being subject to the Romans, did not possess the power to pass or to carry out sentence of death. The Sanhedrin still possessed a great many of its powers, for it was the policy of the Romans to allow their subject countries to go on using their own laws and their own organization, so long as the country was efficiently governed, and so long as peace and good order were maintained; but clearly the right of passing and carrying out sentence of death is something which any government must keep to itself. For that reason, after the trial before the Sanhedrin, Jesus had to be brought before Pilate, the Roman procurator.

It might have been thought that, even if the Jewish court was prejudiced, envenomed and embittered, Jesus would at least have received impartial Roman justice from Pilate, but even that was not to be. The Jewish determination to eliminate Jesus at all costs is seen straight away from the fact that they brought Jesus before Pilate on a charge which had never been extracted in the trial and examination before the Sanhedrin, and which they were well aware was a lie. According to the trial before the Sanhedrin, the crime of which Jesus was guilty was the crime of blasphemy, and it is true that that charge did not wholly disappear, for before Pilate the Jews charged Jesus with declaring that he was the Son of God (John 19.7). But the Jewish authorities well knew that, if they brought Jesus before Pilate on a charge of blasphemy, Pilate would refuse to proceed on a charge which to him would seem nothing more than a domestic religious squabble, and even the outcome of misguided superstition. The charge, therefore, which the Jews levelled against Jesus was that he was a political agitator, that he was perverting the nation, that he was forbidding the Jews to pay their taxes to the Roman Emperor, and that he was setting himself up as a king (Luke 23.2), a charge which they were well aware was quite untrue, but a charge which they equally well knew Pilate was bound to investigate, for the one thing which no Roman governor could ever afford to pass over was the possibility of civil disorder and revolution.

In view of this charge, Pilate began his examination of Jesus with a question to which he well knew the answer, for Pilate was an experienced governor, or he would never have been appointed to the explosive province of Palestine; he knew a revolutionary when he saw one, and he knew at once that Jesus was no political insurrectionist. Pilate asked Jesus if he was the king of the Jews, and Jesus accepted the title, although in no worldly and political sense (Matt. 27.11; Mark 15.2; Luke 23.3-5; John 18.33-37). The fact that Pilate made no attempt whatever to follow up this question, or to press home this charge, shows how well aware he was that there was not a grain of truth in it.

In the presence of Jesus Pilate had an almost frightened

awareness that he was in the presence of one who was no common man and who had a certain unearthly quality in him. Pilate was astonished at the silence with which Jesus greeted the shouted charges of his enemies (Matt. 27.13f.; Mark 15.3-5), and he was afraid when he knew that the charge was also that Jesus had called himself the Son of God (John 19.8).

Pilate was well aware that it was 'envy', bitter and unreasonable ill-will, and not justice or any desire for justice, which had made the Jews bring Jesus before him (Matt. 27.18; Mark 15.10). Again and again and again he demanded to know what Jesus had done, declared that he had found Jesus guilty of no charge, and insisted that he could find no crime in him (Matt. 27.23f.; Mark 15.14; Luke 23.4,14f.,22f.; John 18.38; 19.4). In the end he called for water and washed his hands as a futile symbol of the fact that, though he gave the Jews their way with Jesus, he disclaimed all personal responsibility for his condemnation (Matt. 27.24).

More and more events made it difficult for Pilate to condemn Jesus, even if it was still more difficult for him to let him go. There came to him a message from his wife, whom tradition calls Procula, saying that she had been warned in a dream that Pilate should refuse to have anything to do with the condemnation of this righteous man (Matt. 27.19). In the Apocryphal *Acts of Pilate* it is said that there came a continual stream of witnesses demanding to be allowed to give evidence in favour of Jesus. One man said that he had been an invalid for thirty-eight years and that Jesus had healed him; another said that he had been blind and that Jesus had given him sight; another said that he was bowed and that he had been made straight, another that he had been a leper and that Jesus had cleansed him. And there came a woman called Bernice (Veronica in the Latin), who said that in the crowd she had touched the hem of Jesus' garment and that an issue of blood which had troubled her for ten years was stayed.[1]

Pilate made attempts to release Jesus. He proposed to scourge him, although he had done nothing to deserve scourging, and thus to let him go (Luke 23.16,22). There seems to have been a custom that at the Passover time the Jews had the privilege of having a prisoner released to them at the discretion of the governor. At that time there was in custody a prisoner called Barabbas, a man of violence. *Barabbas* would be from the Aramaic *Bar-Abba*, which means either 'son of the father' or 'son of the teacher'. According to the lost *Gospel according to the Hebrews* his name was *Bar-rabban*, which means 'son of the Rabbi'. It is certain that Barabbas was no sneak-thief or petty criminal, and it may well be that he was a high-born young man, son of some famous family, who had become a Zealot, a popular nationalistic leader, who had been arrested after a career of murder and of violence in his fanatical patriotism. Pilate gave the Jews the choice between the release of Barabbas and the release of Jesus; the only result was an outbreak of half-crazed shouting for the release of Barabbas and the condemnation and crucifixion of Jesus. The impression we get is that of a mob, whipped up to a very frenzy, shouting for the release of Barabbas, shrieking in an almost insane fury for the death of Jesus (Matt. 27.15-18,23f.; Mark 15.6-15; Luke 23.18-25; John 18.40; 19.6,15).

In connection with Barabbas one interesting point emerges. The Syriac and the Armenian Versions of the New Testament, the Codex Koridethi, one of the great early manuscripts, all call Barabbas by the name Jesus Barabbas, a reading which Origen also knew. In Matt. 27.17 Moffatt puts the reading Jesus Barabbas in his text, and the Revised Standard Version, although not putting the reading in the

[1] English Translation by M. R. James, *The Apocryphal New Testament*, pp. 101f.

text, notes that it exists. There is, of course, no doubt that Jesus was a very common name, for 'Jesus' is simply the Greek form of the name 'Joshua'. If this reading is true, and if Jesus was also the first name of Barabbas, two things emerge. First, the cry of the mob is even more dramatic— Jesus Barabbas, not Jesus who is called Christ. Second, it is a strange fact that Jesus Barabbas also may well mean 'Jesus the son of the father'. And the whole incident may well mean, in symbol, that the crowd is always liable to accept the man of violence and war as the son of God rather than the man of gentleness and love, and it would stand for the tragic fact that throughout the centuries men have so often put their trust in war and violence rather than in peace and love to solve the problems of the nation and of the world.

In the apocryphal *Acts of Pilate* there exists what purports to be a report by Pilate to the central government at Rome on the trial and execution of Jesus.

There befell of late a matter of which I myself made trial; for the Jews through envy have punished themselves and their posterity with fearful judgments of their own fault; for whereas their fathers had promised that their God would send out of heaven his holy one who should of right be called their king, and did promise that he would send him upon earth by a virgin; he, then, came when I was governor of Judaea, and they beheld him enlightening the blind, cleansing lepers, healing the palsied, driving devils out of men, raising the dead, rebuking the winds, walking upon the waves of the sea dry-shod, and doing many other wonders, and all the people of the Jews calling him the Son of God: the chief priests, therefore, moved with envy against him, took him and delivered him unto me and brought against him one false accusation after another, saying that he was a sorcerer and did things contrary to their law. But I, believing that these things were so, having scourged him, delivered him unto their will; and they crucified him, and when he was buried they set guards upon him. But while my soldiers watched him he rose again on the third day; yet so much was the malice of the Jews kindled that they gave money to the soldiers, saying: Say ye that his disciples stole away his body. But they, though they took the money, were not able to keep silence concerning that which had come to pass, for they also have testified that they saw him arisen and that they received money from the Jews. And these things have I reported unto thy mightiness for this cause, lest some other should lie unto thee, and thou shouldest deem right to believe the false tales of the Jews.[1]

That letter is quite certainly a fiction, but it is also quite certainly the kind of letter that Pilate might well have written about Jesus. Most revealingly, John says of Pilate that he sought to release Jesus (John 19.12), but in every attempt to release him Pilate came up against the implacable hostility of the Jews. How far that hostility went may be seen from the fact that at the trial of Jesus the Jewish leaders made a statement which it is well-nigh incredible that any Jew should ever have made. When Pilate asked them if they wished him to crucify their king, they answered: 'We have no king but Caesar' (John 19.15). For centuries Jews had been suffering and dying for the very reason that they would give the name king to no earthly person but only to God. In order to get rid of Jesus the Jews were prepared to deny their dearest and their most cherished belief. Nothing that Pilate could do would make them move a fraction of an inch from their irreconcilable hatred of Jesus, and from their grim determination to see him die.

All this is true, but we are compelled to ask one question.

[1] M. R. James, *The Apocryphal New Testament,* p. 146.

Why did Pilate yield to the demands of the Jews? He was the Roman governor. How, then, could he be coerced into condemning one whom he knew to be innocent, and into consciously, though desperately unwillingly, perverting the course of justice? Matthew says that Pilate acted as he did act to avoid a riot, and that is certainly partly true (Matt. 27.24). Mark says that he acted as he did to satisfy the crowd (Mark 15.15), and Luke says that he delivered Jesus to their will (Luke 23.25), which is truer yet. But John says that in the end Pilate was compelled to act as he did, because the Jews said: 'If you release this man, you are not Caesar's friend' (John 19.12). That statement has an atmosphere and flavour of blackmail in it; it is not so much a statement as it is a threat. It is in fact nothing less than an implicit threat to report Pilate to Caesar, for any province could report its governor to the Emperor. The fact is that Pilate had by his conduct laid himself open to precisely this threat.

Palestine was a notoriously explosive province. Pilate became procurator of Palestine in AD 26, with the governor of Syria as his immediate superior. Although we know nothing at all about the life and career of Pilate before he came to Palestine, we can be quite certain that he must have been an experienced soldier and a highly successful administrator or he would never have been appointed to so responsible a position in so difficult a province. From the beginning of his term of office Pilate was in trouble with the Jews, and his actions make it clear that he never understood or even tried to understand them, and that he regarded them with complete contempt.

Josephus tells of his first clash with the Jews. The Roman headquarters in Palestine were not in Jerusalem but in Caesarea. In Jerusalem there was always a detachment of troops to act as guardians of the public peace. They were quartered in the Tower of Antonia which actually over-looked the Temple courts. Roman regimental standards had on them a little metal bust of the reigning Emperor. To the Jews such a bust was anathema, for it was a graven image, and the man whom it represented was held to be a god. The Romans were never unreasonable; they were notably tolerant; and they never looked for trouble. Hitherto, therefore, every Roman commander had marched his troops into Jerusalem without the bust of the Emperor on their standards. Pilate clearly had no intention of pandering to the ridiculous prejudices and superstitions of the Jews, and he marched his troops into Jerusalem with the bust of the Emperor still on their standards, but he did it under cover of night, so that at the moment the Jews did not know that it had happened. The morning came; the Jews awoke to find the Roman standards with the bust of the Emperor in Jerusalem—and in the Tower of Antonia overlooking the very Temple itself. The city was in a turmoil of distress which spread rapidly throughout the whole countryside. Pilate himself was at his headquarters in Caesarea. The Jews sent to Caesarea a deputation humbly beseeching Pilate to remove the standards. Pilate refused. For five days they followed him, prostrating themselves before him; he remained adamant. At last he set up his tribunal, his judgment seat, in the market square, and bade the Jews come at a certain hour, and he would give them an answer. They came. At a given signal they were surrounded by soldiers drawn up three deep, and with their drawn weapons in their hands. Pilate thereupon threatened the Jewish deputation with immediate death, unless they abandoned their entreaties and ceased to disturb him. But they bared their necks and bade the soldiers strike, for they would willingly die rather than see all that they held sacred transgressed. Pilate was baffled by this resolution to keep their laws inviolate; he gave in, and he ordered the standards to be removed. Pilate had recklessly begun by provoking a needless conflict with the Jews—and in the contest of wills he had been worsted.

A worse beginning for a governor it would be hard to imagine.[1]

Pilate had not ended his foolishness. His official residence in Jerusalem was the ancient palace of the Herods. In that palace, as Philo tells us, Pilate displayed certain votive shields to the honour of Tiberius the Emperor. The shields had on them in this case no more than the name of Tiberius, to whom they were dedicated, and the name of Pilate, who dedicated them. It was common to attach such shields or tablets with prayers written on them to the knees of the statues of the gods. Now Tiberius was officially a god, and Caesar-worship was almost what might be called the universal religion of the Roman Empire; but never yet had there been any attempt to introduce Caesar-worship into Palestine; the Romans knew Jewish inflexibility far too well to attempt that. This action of Pilate seemed to the Jews the thin end of the wedge; here was an attempt to introduce the first beginnings of Caesar-worship. They could not bear to think that there was within the holy city a votive tablet to an Emperor who was held to be a god. They besought Pilate to remove the shields. Even the four sons of Herod, whose loyalty to Rome could not be questioned, joined in the supplication. Pilate stubbornly refused to take the shields away. It was here the Jews made their first threat. They threatened to take the matter up with Tiberius—and Pilate was alarmed, for he feared that an embassy to the Emperor on this matter might go on to other matters—'his corruption, his acts of insolence, his rapine, his habit of insulting people, his cruelty, his continual murders of people untried and uncondemned, his never-ending and gratuitous and most grievous inhumanity', as Philo lists his crimes. In spite of his fear Pilate remained adamant. Very courteously and very humbly the Jewish leaders wrote direct to the Emperor Tiberius; and thereupon Tiberius rebuked Pilate sternly,

[1] Josephus, *Antiquities* 18.3.1; *Wars* 2.9.2f.

and ordered him at once to remove the shields from Jerusalem to Caesarea. Once again in a contest of wills with the Jews Pilate was worsted, and this time the Emperor had taken the part of the Jews against him—a dangerous and a threatening precedent.[1]

It seemed curiously impossible for Pilate to treat Jewish principles and feelings with anything other than contempt. The third of his unwise actions concerned the construction of a new aqueduct to improve the water supply of Jerusalem. There could hardly have been a worthier or a more useful undertaking. But to build this aqueduct Pilate raided the resources of the Temple treasury. It may be that Pilate confined his taking of the money to funds which could not in any event have been used for sacred purposes because of the sources from which they had come. But worthy though the object was, and careful as Pilate may have been in his taking it, the Jews were enraged. They congregated in crowds with insistent demands that he should abandon the undertaking; before long the demands turned to violent abuse; and the situation was not far from rioting. To control the situation Pilate surrounded the crowds with soldiers armed, but dressed in civilian clothes, and therefore disguised. They had instructions at a given signal to beat the mob up with staves which they were carrying, but not to use their swords and daggers and not to kill. As the affair turned out, the soldiers used much more force than Pilate had intended. The people were, of course, quite unarmed and were caught totally unawares. Guilty and innocent were alike beaten up, a great number were slain, and still more were wounded. True, the riot was nipped in the bud, the protests were ended, but Pilate had acquired another black mark in the eyes of the Jews.[2]

We may follow Pilate to the end of his governorship. In

[1] Philo, *The Embassy to Caius* 38.
[2] Josephus, *Antiquities* 18.3.2.

AD 35 trouble broke out in Samaria. Samaritan tradition said that the vessels of the Tabernacle had been hidden in Mount Gerizim by Moses. An impostor, who, as Josephus caustically says, 'thought lying a thing of little consequence', emerged, and promised to produce the vessels from where they were hidden. He gained a great following who assembled at the town of Tirabatha, and many of whom were unfortunately bearing arms. Samaria was within Pilate's jurisdiction. He promptly blocked the roads and fell on Tirabatha. Many were immediately slain; many were captured and many of the leaders and the most influential were summarily executed. The Samaritan senate thereupon reported Pilate to his superior, Vitellius, the governor of Syria, accusing him of murdering the prisoners, and pleading that Pilate had used excessive force in a situation in which no rebellion had ever been intended. Vitellius promptly ordered Pilate to Rome to answer to the Emperor Tiberius for the charges made against him; but, before Pilate reached Rome, Tiberius died, and so Pilate vanishes from history with an unfinished story.[1]

There is little doubt that Pilate was blackmailed into giving the Jews their way with Jesus. He was afraid that the Jews would report him for his past misdeeds, as one day the Samaritans were to do, and that he would thus lose his post. Pilate's past rose up before him in the greatest moment of decision in his life. Pilate had to choose between losing his post and abandoning Jesus to the fury of the mob without even a pretence of justice. And Pilate chose to keep his post and to allow Jesus to be murdered.

All through his trial, certain unmistakable things stand out about Jesus.

From the purely human point of view, the most amazing fact of all is his complete absence of resentment. First from

[1]   Josephus, *Antiquities* 18.4.1.

the Jews and then from Pilate he received nothing but the most glaring and intolerable injustice. The laws of his own countrymen and the laws of the Romans were deliberately abrogated to compass his death. In neither court was there even a pretence of justice. Almost anyone else in this world would have bitterly resented such injustice, and would have uttered his resentment in no uncertain terms. Jesus is the supreme example of serenity in the face of injustice.

One of the most extraordinary features of the trial of Jesus is that nowhere in it does he seem to be on trial. At all times he is in control of the situation. In the whole collection of characters there, Jesus alone is in control of himself and the situation. The Jews and their leaders are more than half-crazed with hate; there is in them that which sets a mob on a lynching expedition. Their emotions are out of control. Pilate is the very picture of frustration, like an animal caught in a trap, twisting and turning and quite unable to find any way of escape. Never was any governor less capable of governing, or any ruler more tragically helpless. Alone amidst all the wild, unbalanced hatred and the helpless frustration, Jesus stands serene and calm and in control both of the situation and of himself. The last thing that Jesus ever appears to be is on his defence; rather it is he who stands in judgment.

It is clear that all through the trial Jesus never thought of himself as a victim. There are certain Johannine sayings which, whether they are to be taken as literal and verbatim or not, quite certainly reflect and contain the mind of Jesus. Even before the trial Jesus had said: 'I lay down my life, that I may take it again. No one takes it from me, but I lay it down of my own accord' (John 10.17f.). In this situation Jesus still saw the guiding hand of God. When Pilate sought to remind him that his life was in his hands, Jesus reminded Pilate that he could have possessed no power at all, unless it had been given to him (John 19.10f.). Even amidst that heart-breaking injustice, it was still the conviction of Jesus that he was not the victim of men but the chosen instrument and Servant of God. The happenings of the last days and hours were to Jesus, not fragments in a set of circumstances which were out of control, but events in a drama, whose course and whose culmination were in the hands of God.

9

THE CRUCIFIXION OF JESUS

WHEN we come to think about the Cross, we must indeed put the shoes from off our feet, for the place whereon we stand is holy ground. The extraordinary feature about the narrative of the crucifixion in the Gospels is its reticence. 'When they came to the place that is called The Skull, there they crucified him' (Luke 23.33; see Matt. 27.35; Mark 15.22,24; John 19.17f.). There is no attempt to pile horror on horror and agony on agony; there is no attempt to set out the grim and ghastly details; with a bleak and bare economy of words the Gospel writers simply set down the fact in all its stark simplicity. For them that was enough, for they knew the details and the facts, but for us something more is necessary in order that we may even dimly understand something of what Jesus underwent for us and for all mankind.

Following the verdict of condemnation Jesus was scourged, for scourging was always a prelude to crucifixion (Matt. 27.26; Mark 15.15; Luke 23.16; John 19.1). This was something which Jesus had always foreseen, and which he knew awaited him (Matt. 20.19; Mark 10.34; Luke 18.33). There were few more terrible ordeals than Roman scourging. The victim was stripped, and he was either tied to a pillar in a bent position with his back exposed so that he could not move, or he was stretched rigid upon a frame. The scourge was made of leather thongs studded with sharpened pellets of lead or iron and pieces of bone. It literally ripped a man's back to pieces. Many lost consciousness under the lash; many emerged from the experience raving mad; few were untied from their bonds with spirit still unbroken. This was what Jesus suffered.

He was then handed over to the soldiers that they might make sport of him (Matt. 27.27-29; Mark 15.16-20; John 19.2f.). They made him a crown of thorns and gave him a reed for a sceptre and an old purple cloak for a robe, and mocked him as a king and as a prophet. In the case of the soldiers there was neither malice nor hate; they were simply exercising their right to horse-play with one who was to them a pathetic pretender, a failure who had been condemned to a violent death.

Then there began the procession to Calvary. It always followed the same pattern. The criminal was placed in the centre of a hollow square of four Roman soldiers; in front there walked a herald carrying a board whitened with gypsum with the charge painted in black letters upon it. In the case of Jesus it read: 'This is Jesus, King of the Jews' (Matt. 27.37, but the wording is slightly different in each of the four Gospels; see Mark 15.26; Luke 23.38; John 19.19). According to John, it was written in Hebrew, Latin and Greek, so that all could read it (John 19.20); and it was later to be affixed to Jesus' cross. The criminal was taken to the place of crucifixion by the longest possible way, by the busiest streets, and through as many of them as possible, so that he might be a dreadful warning to any other who might be contemplating some crime; and, as he went, he was lashed and goaded on his way.

The criminal was compelled to carry at least part of his own cross to the place of execution. The upright beam of the cross was called the *stipes*; the cross-beam was called the *patibulum*. If there was a regular place of crucifixion, the upright beam usually stood ready there in its socket, and it was the cross-beam, the *patibulum*, which the prisoner had to carry. Sometimes the *patibulum* consisted of one single beam; more often, perhaps, it consisted of a double beam joined at one end and open at the other, and the prisoner's head was fitted into the space between the two beams. The exhausting experiences of the night of trials and examinations, and the terrible torture of the scourging, had left Jesus so weak that he staggered and fell under the weight of the beam, and Simon of Cyrene, no doubt a pilgrim to the Passover from North Africa, had the grim experience of being all unexpectedly impressed into the Roman service in order to carry the cross (Matt. 27.32; Mark 15.21; Luke 23.26). Palestine was an occupied country, and a Roman officer had only to touch a Jew on the shoulder with the flat of the blade of a spear to compel him to submit to any service, however menial and however repulsive. It is said that they *brought* Jesus to the place called Golgotha (Mark 15.22). In the best manuscripts the word used for 'to bring' is *pherein*, which most naturally means to bear or to carry; and it may well be that Jesus had to be carried and supported to the cross. On the way to the cross there followed Jesus those who had loved him and who mourned for him, and Luke tells how he warned them of still worse things to come (Luke 23.27-31).

When the place of crucifixion was reached, the cross was laid flat on the ground and the criminal was then laid on top of it. At this point it was the custom to give to the victim a drink of medicated wine, which was mercifully prepared by a group of pious women in Jerusalem in obedience to the command of Prov. 31.6: 'Give strong drink to him who is perishing, and wine to those in bitter distress'. The medicated wine was an opiate to dull the pain, but Jesus tasted it and then refused to accept it, for he would meet death at its bitterest and with all his senses at their keenest (Matt. 27.34; Mark 15.23). Half-way up the upright beam of the cross there was a projecting ledge of wood, called the saddle, on which part of the weight of the criminal's body rested, or the weight of his body would have torn the nails clean through his hands. As the criminal was stretched upon the cross, the nails were driven through his hands. Frequently at that moment victims cursed and swore and shrieked and spat at their executioners, but it was then that Jesus prayed: 'Father, forgive them; for they know not what they do' (Luke 23.34). Then in a moment of searing agony the cross was lifted up and set in its socket with the victim hanging on it.

Before the criminal was nailed to the cross—usually only the hands were nailed and the feet were only loosely bound to the upright—the criminal had been stripped save for a loin cloth, which was left to him for decency's sake. The clothes of the criminal were the perquisite of the detachment of four soldiers in charge of the crucifixion. A Jew wore six articles of clothing; there were the belt, the sandals, the girdle, the turban and the tunic, which were of almost equal value, and in the distribution of which there would be no real difficulty. But the main article of clothing was a great robe which served a man as a cloak by day and a blanket by night, and which was so essential an article of clothing that the law laid it down that, even if it was taken for debt, it must be returned to a man at night that he might sleep in it (Ex. 22.26f.). Jesus' robe was specially finely made, for it was woven without seam. Clearly to have cut it up would have been to ruin it, so the soldiers cast lots beneath the cross to see which of them was to have it (Matt. 27.35; Mark 15.24; Luke 23.34; John 19.23f.).

From the cross Jesus was watching. The cross was not high, only from seven to nine feet high at the highest, and he could easily see what was happening. Now there was a Jewish custom in regard to the great outer robe. It was not in shops that clothes were bought in those days; they were made at home. It was the mother who wove the cloth and cut and sewed and shaped it; and usually, before a son left home to go out into the world, his mother's last gift to him was a great outer robe, woven and made with her own hands. No doubt it was Mary who had woven the robe of Jesus, and Jesus' thoughts turned to his mother, and to her lone- liness in the days to come. The disciple whom Jesus loved was standing watching there. 'Woman,' said Jesus to Mary, 'behold your son!' And to the beloved disciple he said: 'Behold your mother!' (John 19.26f.).

Not even on the cross would the venom of Jesus' enemies leave him alone. Even there they taunted him. What an end for him who claimed to be the Son of God! What an end for a king! What an end to the would-be destroyer and rebuilder of the Temple! A strange saviour who offered to save others and who was powerless to save himself! (Matt. 27.39-43; Mark 15.29-32; Luke 23.35-37). They came to gloat over the man whom they thought that they were eliminating from life for ever.

On that day Jesus was not the only victim. Two brigands were crucified with him (Matt. 27.38; Mark 15.27; Luke 23.32; John 19.18). Matthew says that they too joined in the mockery. They were not robbers in the sense of petty criminals, or burglars, or sneak-thieves; they were *lēstai*, which means 'brigands', and doubtless they were reckless adventurers and outlaws and men of courage, even if they had taken to a career of crime. But Luke tells us that one of them was fascinated by Jesus even on the cross; he rebuked his fellow-brigand, reminding him that they deserved their fate, while Jesus was guiltless. Then he made one of the most amazing statements in all history. To a broken Galilaean hanging in agony on a cross, mocked by the orthodox among his countrymen, an apparent failure if ever there was one, that brigand said: 'Jesus, remember me when you come in your kingly power.' And back came the calm, strong voice of Jesus: 'Today you will be with me in

Paradise' (Luke 23.39-43). It is hardly possible that the world ever saw a less likely candidate for a kingdom, yet in Jesus that brigand saw a king, and Jesus accepted his homage.

It was at 'the third hour'—that is, at nine o'clock in the morning, for, as we have seen, the twelve hours of the Jewish day were counted from 6 a.m. to 6 p.m.—that Jesus had been crucified. When the sun was at its zenith, instead of the brightness of noon there came upon the land a darkness as of midnight, settling on Jerusalem for the next three hours (Matt. 27.45; Mark 15.33; Luke 23.44f.). At three o'clock in the afternoon the most terrible of all cries was wrung from Jesus: 'My God, my God, why hast thou forsaken me?' (Matt. 27.46; Mark 15.34). At that moment Jesus was plumbing unfathomable depths for us men and for our salvation.

And now the drama was coming to its close. Parched by his agony, Jesus said: 'I thirst', and a soldier in a moment of mercy gave him a drink of the rough vinegar wine which was all that the soldiers were allowed to drink when they were on duty (Matt. 27.48; Mark 15.36; John 19.28f.).

The end was very near. Jesus uttered a loud cry (Matt. 27.50; Mark 15.37; Luke 23.46). That cry was neither a cry of pain nor yet a cry of despair. It was a cry of triumph: 'It is finished' (John 19.30), which in Jesus' own tongue was one triumphant word. And then he prayed. He prayed the first prayer that every Jewish boy was taught to pray by his mother before the dark came down; he prayed the prayer that Mary had taught him when he was a little boy: 'Father, into thy hands I commit my spirit' (Luke 23.46; Ps. 31.5). Then he bowed his head and died, and the word which John uses when he says that Jesus *bowed* his head (*klinein*) is the word which would be used for a man peacefully letting his head sink back upon his pillow that he might sleep. And so there came the peace after the long battle, the rest after the bitter toil, the ease after the agony.

At that moment the curtain which veiled the Holy of Holies in the Temple was rent in two (Matt. 27.51; Mark 15.38; Luke 23.45); and at that moment the centurion who was in charge of the crucifixion was kneeling before the cross, breathing out in wonder: 'Truly this was a son of God' (Matt. 27.54; Mark 15.39; Luke 23.47). Jesus, lifted up from the earth, had drawn the first of his captives to himself in the very moment of his death.

In all the agony there was only one mercy. The terror of crucifixion was that it was a lingering death. A man might hang on a cross for days, tortured by the flies, parched with thirst, burned by the sun, frozen by the night frosts, until he died raving mad. If a man refused to die, it was the custom to pound him to death with blows of a mallet. The next day was the Sabbath, and before the Sabbath the bodies must be taken down. At the request of the Jews the soldiers took steps to hasten the end. The brigands were pounded to death; but mercifully Jesus was dead. They plunged a spear into his side and there came out water and blood; so the divine tragedy was ended (John 19.31-35).

We must now go on to look at Jesus on the Cross in order to see what that picture tells us simply and non-theologically about him.

On the Cross we see *the courage of Jesus*. Of all deaths crucifixion is the most terrible. It can involve a man in a death which is a lingering agony. In his article on crucifixion in Smith's *Dictionary of the Bible*, F. W. Farrar quotes from the work of a physician called Richter who wrote a treatise on the physical effects of crucifixion. The unnatural position and the tension of the body made every movement a pain. The fact that the nails were driven through those parts of the hands where the nerves and the tendons are, made every movement the most exquisite torture. The wounds of the nails and the weals of the lash very soon became inflamed and even gangrenous. The position of the body hindered the circulation, and caused a pain and tension in the body which is described as more intolerable than death itself. The agony of crucifixion was the worst kind of agony, lingering, gradually but inevitably increasing every moment. And to all this must be added the burning thirst which soon began to torture the victim. These are not pleasant facts, but this was crucifixion—and Jesus knew it. Crucifixion was by no means an uncommon penalty for evil-doers and revolutionaries in Palestine. In the unrest which followed the death of Herod the Great, Varus, the Roman general, captured Sepphoris in Galilee and lined the roads of Galilee with no fewer than two thousand crosses.[1] That was a story that Jesus must often have heard; he must have known well, and may perhaps even have seen, the agony of crucifixion. Jesus knew what crucifixion was like; to the end he might have escaped from it; yet he went steadily on, and in the end he even refused the opiate offered in mercy (Matt. 27.34) that he might endure pain to the uttermost, and that he might meet death with steady eyes and with mind unclouded. It is one kind of courage to do some gallant action on the spur of the moment before there is even time to think. It is another and a far higher kind of courage to know that there is agony and torture at the end of a chosen road, and to go steadily on to meet it.

On the Cross we see *the humanity of Jesus*. There have always been those in the Church who in a false reverence have been unwilling and unable to take the manhood of Jesus seriously. Such people were known as the Docetists, which means, as we might put it, the Seemists. Christianity came into a world in which the body was despised, in which the spirit was all-important, and in which a man was held

[1] Josephus, *Antiquities* 17.10.10.

to be able to reach truth and light and God only when he had sloughed off the body. *Sōma sēma* ran the popular saying, the body is a tomb. Plotinus could say that he was ashamed that he had a body. Epictetus could describe himself as a poor soul shackled to a corpse. Seneca could talk of the 'detestable habitation' of the body. The result was that there were those who held that the body of Jesus was only a phantom and an appearance and in no sense a real body. 'The blood of Christ,' said Jerome, 'was still fresh in Jerusalem when his body was said to be a phantasm.'[1] Ignatius continually inveighs against those who held that Jesus only *seemed* to suffer. In the apocryphal *Acts of John* it is said that the feet of Jesus left no print on the ground when he walked, and that his body was immaterial to the touch. That same book tells how at the very time of the crucifixion Jesus met John on the Mount of Olives, and told him that he only *seemed* to suffer on Calvary, but in reality he was with John.[2] Many of the Gnostic Docetists held that the divine Christ came into the man Jeşus at the Baptism and left him before the crucifixion, so that, while the man Jesus did suffer, the divine Christ suffered not at all. Basilides taught that in fact it was not Jesus but Simon of Cyrene who was crucified, although he looked like Jesus, while Jesus stood by and laughed. Jesus was held to have a 'psychic' body, not subject to the laws of matter, not subject to any human desire, passion, or emotion, and quite incapable of feeling pain. It was said that, when his body was taken down from the cross, it was nothing but a 'void'. But the crucifixion narrative in the Gospels unmistakably sets before us the humanity of Jesus. We see Jesus stagger and faint beneath the weight of the beam of the cross; we see him in his human pain and weakness having to be half-carried to Calvary. We hear the human cry: 'I thirst' (John 19.28f.). We hear Pilate's 'Here is the man!' (John 19.5).

[1] *Against the Luciferians* 23.   [2] *Acts of John* 93, 97.

One of the great aims of the story of the Cross is to show the real and full manhood of Jesus and the complete reality of his sufferings. Here is no phantasm of a body, but quivering human flesh; here is no acted appearance of suffering, but a terrible reality of agony.

On the Cross we see *the identity of Jesus with sinners*. That is symbolically marked in his crucifixion between two criminals (Matt. 27.38; Mark 15.27; Luke 23.33; John 19.18). It was said of the Suffering Servant in Isaiah: 'They made his grave with the wicked . . . He was numbered with the transgressors' (Isa. 53.9,12). Jesus had always been the friend of tax-gatherers and sinners (Matt. 11.19), a friendship which had shocked the orthodox of his day (Matt. 9.10-13). It is symbolic of his whole work that he was crucified between two criminals and identified with sinners in his death.

On the Cross we see *the invincible forgiveness of Jesus*. Even as they drove the nails through him, he prayed: 'Father, forgive them; for they know not what they do' (Luke 23.34). It is as if Jesus said: 'No matter what you do to me, I will still forgive.' If in Jesus we see the mind of God fully displayed, it means that there are no limits to the love, the grace, the forgiveness of God. We see Jesus on the Cross embodying the message of divine forgiveness which he brought to men.

On the Cross we see *the selflessness of Jesus*. Even in his own agony he remembered the sorrow and the loneliness of Mary, and committed her to the care of the disciple whom he loved (John 19.26f.). Nothing is more extraordinary in the whole story of Jesus than his absolute refusal to use his powers for his own gain, his own profit, his own comfort, or his own safety. He thought never in terms of self, and always in terms of others.

On the Cross we see *the depths which Jesus plumbed* in his complete identification with the human situation. 'My

God, my God,' he said, 'why hast thou forsaken me?' (Matt. 27.46; Mark 15.34). There are many of Jesus' sayings which are uninventable, but this one is supremely such.

It is sometimes held that, when Jesus said this, he was beginning to quote Ps. 22, which begins with these very words; and, indeed, that Psalm seems inextricably interwoven with the events of the Cross. The Psalmist, describing his own evil case, goes on: 'All who see me mock at me; they make mouths at me, they wag their heads; "He committed his cause to the Lord, let him deliver him; let him rescue him, for he delights in him"' (vv. 7f.). Still describing his experiences the Psalmist goes on: 'They divide my garments among them, and for my raiment they cast lots' (v. 18). But the Psalm ends not in tragedy but in triumph: 'He has not despised or abhorred the affliction of the afflicted; and he has not hid his face from him, but has heard when he cried to him. From thee comes my praise in the great congregation; my vows I will pay before those who fear him. The afflicted shall eat and be satisfied; those who seek him shall praise the Lord! May your hearts live for ever!' (vv. 24-26). So it has been suggested that this saying of Jesus is not so much, as it were, a personal saying, but that it is rather the beginning of the psalm, which Jesus was quoting to himself to remind himself of the servant of God in the ancient times who had begun in shame and humiliation and who had ended in confidence and glory.

But, as we have said before, it may well be that this is the cry of Jesus caught up in a situation which he knew God intended him to go through, but which he could not understand, that here is Jesus going through the darkness of having to accept that which he did not understand—which is so often an essential part of the human situation. It could never have been claimed that Jesus fully knew the human situation unless he experienced that.

On the Cross we see *the royalty of Jesus*. Again and again

we are confronted with the fact that at no time did Jesus seem a broken figure, a victim of circumstances; at all times he carried himself like a king. It was to this man on the cross that the crucified brigand appealed as to a king for a place in his kingdom. John Buchan in his biography of Montrose tells how Montrose was finally captured and brought to Edinburgh for trial and execution. As the procession passed up the Canongate the street was lined with crowds, 'the dregs of the Edinburgh slums, the retainers of the Covenanting lords, ministers from far and near'. The crowds had been deliberately incited, and had even been supplied with ammunition, to stone Montrose as he passed. But the strange thing was that somehow that day in Edinburgh not a voice was raised, not a hand was lifted, not a missile was thrown. The crowd gazed silent and fascinated on one who was treated as a criminal but who looked like a king. 'It is absolutely certain,' wrote one who witnessed the scene, 'that he hath overcome more men by his death in Scotland than he would have done, if he had lived. For I never saw a more sweeter carriage in a man in all my life.' There have always been some men whose kingliness nothing can obscure. Jesus was supremely and uniquely such. Even in the dying criminal on the cross the brigand saw a king.

On the Cross we see *the peace of Jesus*. He died with the child's good-night prayer upon his lips (Luke 23.46; Ps. 31.5). He died as one laying his head upon a pillow to sleep (John 19.30). He died not like a disappointed man with a broken heart, but like one well content that his work was done.

On the Cross we see *the triumph of Jesus*. It is with the cry of victory, 'It is finished,' that he died (John 19.30). His task was accomplished and his work was done, and already in the astonished centurion the Cross had begun its triumphs.

10

LOOKING AT THE CROSS

No one will deny that the Cross is designed to awaken within us not theological disputation but adoring love. It is nevertheless true that the more we think about the Cross and the more we understand it, the greater will be the love and adoration within our hearts. The obligation is, therefore, laid upon us to seek to understand at least something of what happened on the Cross for all mankind and for us. As we read the narrative of the Gospels certain things become unmistakably clear.

(i) It is clear that Jesus went willingly, spontaneously and open-eyed to the Cross. There have been those who saw in Jesus' life 'the Galilaean spring time', a time when men responded to him and when he expected good success. Slowly, it is suggested, Jesus came to see that men would finally and totally reject him, and that there was no other way than the way of the Cross. On that view Jesus went to the Cross because circumstances compelled him to do so, but the Cross was not his original plan. But, if we place any reliance on the story of the Gospels, there never was a time in his earthly life when Jesus was not aware that at the end of the road there stood the Cross. We can trace this consciousness of Jesus backwards through the story.

(a) Towards the very end of his ministry there was the woman who in Bethany anointed Jesus with the very precious ointment. There were those who regarded this act of love as an extravagant waste, but Jesus bade them to let her alone, because she had done it, as it were, to prepare him for burial (Matt. 26.12; Mark 14.8). By this time Jesus had not the slightest doubt that he must die.

(*b*) Shortly before that incident Jesus had spoken the parable of the wicked husbandmen (Matt. 21.33-46; Mark 12.1-12; Luke 20.9-18). The dramatic culmination of that parable is the murder of the heir by the husbandmen, and it is plain that Jesus was foretelling what was to happen to himself. Again he was in no doubt that death awaited him, and violent death.

(*c*) Following upon Peter's great discovery and confession at Caesarea Philippi Jesus repeatedly foretold his own death. 'And he began to teach them that the Son of Man must suffer many things, and be rejected by the elders and the chief priests and the scribes, and be killed, and after three days rise again' (Mark 8.31f.; 9.31f.; 10.33f.; Matt. 16.21; 17.22; Luke 9.22,44). Denney rightly calls attention to the tense of the verbs in Mark 9.31. The verbs for *to teach* and *to say* are both in the imperfect tense (*edidasken* and *elegen*), and that tense expresses repeated, habitual and continuous action. From that time on Jesus repeatedly and openly spoke to his disciples about his coming death on the Cross.

(*d*) Early in the narrative of the Gospels there is an incident which all three synoptic Gospels relate. The disciples of the Pharisees came asking why the disciples of Jesus did not fast as they did. Jesus' answer was that, so long as the bridegroom was with them, the wedding guests could not fast, but, that a day would come when the bridegroom would be taken away from them, and then they would fast (Matt. 9.14f.; Mark 2.18f.; Luke 5.33f.). Jesus clearly foretold that the joy of fellowship would be followed by the grief of separation.

(*e*) We can trace the matter even further back than that. At the moment of his baptism the divine voice said to Jesus:

'Thou art my beloved Son; with thee I am well pleased' (Mark 1.11; Matt. 3.17; Luke 3.22). That saying is composed of two quotations from the Old Testament. 'Thou art my beloved Son,' is a quotation of Ps. 2.7. That Psalm is a coronation Psalm, and was always taken as pointing to the triumph and enthronement of the Messiah. 'With thee I am well pleased,' is a quotation from Isa. 42.1, and is part of the description of the Servant of the Lord, whose portrait finds its culmination in the picture of one who was wounded for our transgressions and bruised for our iniquities in Isa. 53. This can only mean that from the beginning Jesus thought of himself in terms of the messianic office, but also thought of himself in terms of the Suffering Servant of the Lord.

Here, then, is the first thing which we can say with confidence of the Cross of Jesus. Jesus was not driven to the Cross by force of circumstances. The Cross was not an afterthought when some original hope and plan and scheme had been disappointed. From the beginning Jesus voluntarily and spontaneously thought in terms of the Cross. The Fourth Gospel correctly interprets the mind of Jesus when it pictures him as saying: 'I lay down my life that I may take it again. No one takes it from me, but I lay it down of my own accord' (John 10.17f.).

(ii) Although Jesus voluntarily accepted the Cross, it is also true that he looked on the Cross as an utter necessity. He did not regard his death as the result of some uncontrolled concatenation of circumstances, or as some accidental happening. He regarded it as necessary and essential. 'The Son of Man,' he said, '*must* (*dei*) suffer many things . . . and be killed' (Mark 8.31; Matt. 16.21; Luke 9.22). 'The Son of Man goes as it has been determined' (Luke 22.22). To Jesus the Cross was something which was an essential happening from which there was no escape.

(iii)   How is it that Jesus could regard the Cross at one and the same time as his own voluntary and spontaneous choice and an utter necessity? The answer is that Jesus was certain that the Cross was part of the eternal will and purpose of God. In Gethsemane Jesus was struggling not to discover God's will, but to accept God's will (Matt. 26.36-46; Mark 14.32-42; Luke 22.39-46). Jesus, therefore, did not regard himself as the victim of men, but as the agent and instrument and willing servant of God. He saw the Cross not as the necessity of an iron determinism or an inescapable fate, but as part of the plan and the purpose and the design of God. It was, therefore, something which was at one and the same time voluntary and essential, for the will of Jesus was fully and perfectly and voluntarily identified with the will of God, his Father. In one sense escape lay open to him. He need never have come to Jerusalem. He could have compromised with the orthodox Jewish leaders. Regiments of angels were his for his defence, if he had wished it so (Matt. 26.51-54). But in another sense there was no such thing as escape for him, for there could never be escape from the will of God.

For Jesus, then, the Cross was completely voluntary, absolutely essential, and an integral part of the will and purpose of God.

The meaning of Jesus is something which a man must always discover for himself. The basic question of Jesus is: 'Who do *you* say that I am?' (Matt. 16.15; Mark 8.29; Luke 9.20). It is not enough to quote what others have said about Jesus. Personal knowledge, personal confrontation, personal discovery and personal decision alone are enough. But, although that is so, we despoil ourselves of something which is of infinite preciousness and value, if we disregard the thoughts and discoveries of those who have gone out on the adventure of thought before us. We will, therefore, do well to see how others have interpreted the Cross and the death of Jesus.

The basic New Testament statement about the death of Jesus and its significance is the saying of Paul: 'Christ died for our sins in accordance with the scriptures' (I Cor. 15.3). It is important to remember what the word *for* means in this statement. The word is *huper*, and it does not mean *because of* or *in place of*. It means *on behalf of, for the sake of*, a fact which only Kenneth Wuest of all the modern translators brings out. The meaning is that Jesus Christ died in order to do something on behalf of our sins. That is to say, our sins and the death of Jesus Christ are indissolubly connected.

The Church in its wisdom has never had any official and orthodox doctrine of the Atonement. Wisely the Church has left every man to find his own way to salvation through the life and death of Jesus. But we can go one step further in company, before the ways diverge. The word atonement is really *at-one-ment*. We may, therefore, go on to say that the death of Jesus has done something which nothing else could ever do to make us *at one* with God. However we go on to interpret these basic statements—and the interpretations of them are many—we must begin with the two great kindred facts that Jesus died on behalf of the sins of men, and the effect of his death is to remove the estrangement between man and God and to make man and God *at one*.

(i) The simplest view of the work of Jesus Christ is that he lived and died to be our example. 'Christ also suffered for you,' wrote Peter, 'leaving you an example, that you should follow in his steps' (I Peter 2.21). The word for example is *hupogrammos*, which is the word for the perfect line of copperplate handwriting at the top of the page of a child's writing exercise-book, the line which he must copy and which he must seek to reproduce. Jesus, then, in his life and death left us an example which we must reproduce. Even in so great a passage as Phil. 2.1-11 in which Paul speaks so lyrically about the self-emptying of Jesus Christ for the sake of men, that self-emptying and that sacrificial obedience are set out as an example of the mind and heart and conduct which should be in the Christian. When Clement of Rome was writing to the warring church at Corinth, he quoted Isa. 53 at length to show what the Servant of the Lord must be like, and then he went on to say: 'You see, beloved, what is the example which is given to us, for, if the Lord was thus humble-minded, what shall we do, who through him have come under the yoke of grace?'[1] When Polycarp was writing to the Philippians, he spoke about the sufferings of Jesus for mankind, and then he went on to say: 'Let us then be imitators of his endurance, and, if we suffer for his name's sake, let us glorify him. For this is the example which he gave us in himself, and this is what we have believed.'[2] Irenaeus speaks of the Christians as 'imitators of his works as well as doers of his words'.[3] Lactantius thinks of Jesus as the perfect teacher, teaching not only by precept but by example. The teacher must practise what he teaches and must 'hold out his hand to one who is about to follow him'. 'It is befitting,' he says, 'that a master and teacher of virtue should most closely resemble man, that by overpowering sin, he may teach man that sin may be overpowered by him.' And if man should answer that the task is impossible, then this Jesus, who was real human flesh and blood, makes answer: 'See, I myself do it.'[4] Augustine in one of his earlier works describes the whole life of Jesus, as H. E. W. Turner translates the phrase, as 'a moral instruction', *disciplina morum*.[5] The idea of the work of Jesus as example is deeply rooted in Christian thought.

---

[1] *I Clement* 16.17. [2] *To the Philippians* 8.2. [3] *Against Heresies* 5.1.1. [4] *Divine Institutes* 4.24. [5] Augustine, *On True Religion* 16.32; H. E. W. Turner, *The Patristic Doctrine of Redemption*, p. 35.

Closely allied with the idea of Jesus as the perfect example
is the idea of him as the divine bringer of knowledge, the
divine illuminer of men, the divine revealer of God and the
truth of God. As the New Testament itself has it, we have
'the light of the knowledge of the glory of God in the face
of Christ' (II Cor. 4.6). He brings us the truth and the truth
makes us free (John 8.32). He brings life and immortality to
light through his glorious gospel (II Tim. 1.10).

The early Church loved to dwell on the thought of the
knowledge, the illumination, the revelation which came in
Jesus Christ. It is for 'the life and knowledge' which were
made known through Jesus that the Eucharistic prayer of
the *Didache* gives thanks.[1] Jesus Christ, says Ignatius, is
the word of God 'proceeding from silence'.[2] 'Through him,'
writes Clement of Rome, 'we fix our gaze on the heights of
heaven, through him we see the reflection of his faultless
and lofty countenance, through him the eyes of our hearts
were opened, through him our foolish and darkened understanding blossoms towards the light, through him the Master
willed that we should taste immortal knowledge.'[3] Through
him God called us 'from darkness to light, from ignorance
to the full knowledge of the glory of his name'.[4] Through
Jesus Christ, writes Lactantius, 'the fountain of God, most
abundant and most full, is open to all; and this heavenly
light rises for all, as many as have eyes'.[5] 'In no other way,'
says Irenaeus, 'could we have learned the things of God,
unless our Master, existing as the Word, had become man.'
In him the invisible becomes visible, the incomprehensible is
made comprehensible, the impassible becomes capable of
suffering.[6]

In the New Testament itself we have the great picture of
Jesus Christ the example, the illuminer, the revealer. Clearly

---

[1] *Didache* 9.3; 10.2.   [2] *To the Magnesians* 8.2.   [3] *I Clement*
36.2.   [4] *I Clement* 59.2.   [5] *Divine Institutes* 3.26.
[6] *Against Heresies* 5.1.1.; 3.16.6.

the work of Jesus Christ, the atonement he made, must mean more than that, if for no other reason than that example without the power to follow it, knowledge without the power to put it into practice, revelation without the power to turn it into life, can bring nothing but bitter frustration. And yet it remains true, as H. E. W. Turner writes, of this conception of the work of Jesus that 'No doctrine of the Cross . . . which does not explain how the world is made better by it can claim to represent the fulness of the Christian tradition. Again, any theory which separates the obligation of leading a better life from the redemption brought by Christ has small claim for acceptance by Christians.'[1]

(ii)   Another of the great early Church conceptions of the work of Jesus Christ is expressed in the idea of *recapitulation*. Strange as this conception may now seem to us, it was one of the great basic conceptions of Irenaeus. It finds its biblical basis in three passages. In Eph. 1.10 the aim of God is said to be, as the Authorized Version translates it, 'to gather together all things in Christ'. The Revised Standard Version translates it 'to unite all things in Christ'. The Twentieth Century New Testament translates it 'to make all things centre in Christ'. The word in Greek is *anakephalaiousthai*. Now this word could have another sense; it could mean to summarize, to recapitulate, as it were, to make a *précis* of. It is in this sense that Irenaeus takes it. The other two Scripture passages which are the basis of this conception are Rom. 5 and I Cor. 15.21f., where there is a close parallel drawn between Adam and Christ. 'As by a man came death, by a man has come also the resurrection of the dead. For as in Adam all die, so also in Christ shall all be made alive.'

To put it very simply, the idea is that Jesus Christ recapitulates, re-enacts, reiterates, repeats the whole course of human history in himself with this crucial difference—

[1] *The Patristic Doctrine of Redemption*, p. 46.

that he at all times presents the perfect life and the perfect obedience which man ought to have offered and failed to offer. By so doing Jesus Christ reverses the whole course of human history; he makes it what it ought to be; he cancels out the sins and the failures and the rebellions and the disobediences. He thus by living life as it ought to be, redeems man from the consequence of his sins. Jesus Christ repeats human history in the way it ought to have gone.

Jesus Christ, as Irenaeus puts it, became incarnate and was made man, and in himself he recapitulated the long line of human beings ... so that what we had lost in Adam we recover in Jesus Christ.[1] Jesus Christ recapitulates God's handiwork in himself (4.6.2). By recapitulating things in himself Jesus, as it were, begins a new creation, this time without sin (5.23.2). Jesus Christ recapitulates the disobedience which came from a tree in the Garden of Eden by the obedience of the tree on which he hung on Calvary (5.19.1). In the same way Mary recapitulated in obedience the disobedience of Eve, and so becomes what has been called 'a subsidiary champion' of the human race (3.22.4).

The idea is that Jesus Christ recapitulates in himself the whole story and the whole drama of human history; he recapitulates the whole human struggle with temptation and with sin; but there is this vital difference: where in man the story had gone wrong, in Jesus Christ everything is right, and thereby man is redeemed from his sin and from the consequences of it.

In one sense this is a conception which is utterly strange to the modern mind. It depends on the ancient idea of racial solidarity. Because of this idea of solidarity Adam's sin became the sin of the whole human race, and Christ's goodness became the goodness of the whole human race. In another sense this may well be called the most modern of all conceptions of the work of Christ. It could be expressed

[1] *Against Heresies* 3.18.1.

in modern times in this way. Through man's disobedience the process of the evolution of the human race went wrong, and the course of its wrongness and its error could neither be halted nor reversed by any human means. But in Jesus Christ the whole course of human evolution was perfectly carried out and realized in obedience to the purpose of God; he is the man God meant all men to be. He recapitulates human history, realizing the ideal instead of losing the ideal, and so redeems humanity from its sin.

(iii)　One of the great dominant pictures of the work of Jesus Christ in his life and in his death, both in the New Testament and in the thought of the early Church, is the picture of Christ the Victor, the *Christus Victor* theme as it has been called. This is the idea that in his life and in his death and in his resurrection Jesus finally and utterly defeated the evil demonic powers whose aim was to compass the death and destruction of men.

This was a conception of the work of Jesus Christ which was intensely real and vivid to Jew and to Greek, to Christian and to pagan alike, for both alike had no doubt as to the existence of these malignant demons. 'It is not we alone who speak of wicked demons,' wrote Origen to Celsus, 'but it is almost all who acknowledge the existence of demons.'[1]

The ancient world was a haunted world. 'It is hard, perhaps,' says H. E. W. Turner, 'for modern man to realize how hag-ridden was the world into which Christ came.'[2] 'The whole world,' says Harnack, 'and the circumambient atmosphere were filled with devils . . . They sat on thrones, they hovered round cradles. The world was literally a hell.'[3] Plutarch in his treatise *On Superstition* spoke of the craven fear of God 'filling the universe with spectres'.

The Jews believed intensely in demons. The demons were either the spirits of the wicked departed, still malignantly

---

[1]　*Against Celsus* 7.69.　　[2]　*The Patristic Doctrine of Redemption*, p. 47.　　[3]　*The Expansion of Christianity I*, p. 161.

working evil, or they were the descendants of the union of the sinful angels and mortal women in the old story in Gen. 6.4. According to Jewish belief there were tens of thousands of demons, living in unclean places, lurking in tombs and in places where there was no water, howling in the deserts. They ever threatened the lonely traveller, the little child, the woman in childbirth, those newly married. It was the demons who got into a man's body and mind and caused mental and physical illness. There was an Egyptian belief that there were thirty-six parts in the body and any of them might be occupied by a malignant demon.[1] *Mazzikin* they were called, those who work harm.

The Greeks no less believed in demons. Plutarch, writing on the mysteries of Isis, suggested that 'these sinister spirits assert their vast power, and display their malevolence, not only in plague, pestilence and dearth, and all the desolating convulsions of the physical world, but in the moral perversion and deception of the human race'. He suggested that each of the blessed gods had attached to him an evil demon, who in the god's name perpetrated every kind of enormity, masquerading as a god.[2] For Jew and Greek the world was in bondage to the spirits of evil.

Belief in these demons was part of the faith and even of the instruction of the Christian Church. They are 'the principalities and powers' whom we meet in the New Testament. 'I myself,' writes Ignatius, 'though I am in bonds . . . can understand heavenly things, and the places of the angels and gatherings of the principalities.'[3] It is from fear of the principalities and powers that Christ relieves us (Rom. 8.38). It is against principalities and powers that the Christian soldier wrestles (Eph. 6.12). And then there comes the tremendous triumphant claim of what Christ did on the

[1] Origen, *Against Celsus* 7.58.
[2] S. Dill, *Roman Society from Nero to Marcus Aurelius,* pp. 431f.
[3] *To the Trallians* 5.2.

Cross. 'He disarmed the principalities and powers and made a public example of them, triumphing over them in it' (Col. 2.15). The idea is that on the Cross there was a death grapple between Jesus Christ and the demonic powers of evil, and that once and for all their power was finally defeated and broken. To us this may seem very remote, but to that haunted ancient world there was nothing more wonderful and amazing than to be able to believe that the power of the demons was broken for ever.

H. E .W. Turner[1] summarizes the way in which Martin Werner works out how, not simply the Cross, but every part of Jesus' life was operative in this victory over the powers of evil.

It began at his birth. Ignatius says that by the rising of the wondrous star 'all magic was dissolved, and every bond of wickedness vanished away, ignorance was removed, and the old kingdom was destroyed, when God became manifest as man'.[2] Origen has the idea that it was precisely because their magic and incantations and spells were no longer effective that the Magi knew that there had entered into the world a 'greater manifestation of divinity', by which the powers of the evil spirits were overthrown. They knew that now there had come into the world and there had broken into life some one superior to all the demons.[3]

It is easy to see how the temptation narrative can be used to show the victorious battle of Jesus against the assailing powers of evil.

On the Cross there came the great victorious battle in which the power of the demons was broken for ever. If the 'world rulers', that is, the demons had known what they were doing, and what they were bringing on themselves, they would not have crucified Christ (I Cor. 2.8). On the Cross

---

[1] *The Patristic Doctrine of Redemption,* pp. 49-52.
[2] *To the Ephesians* 19.2.
[3] *Against Celsus* 1.69.

Jesus Christ became the slayer of death himself. Cyril of Jerusalem vividly writes: 'Death was struck with dismay on beholding a new visitant descend into Hades, not bound with the chains of that place.'[1]

Clearly this victory becomes even more complete and evident in the event of the Resurrection. 'Through his resurrection,' says Origen, 'he destroyed the kingdom of death, whence it is written that he freed captivity.'[2]

Equally clearly, the descent into Hades is a part of the victorious progress of Jesus Christ. The *Gospel of Nicodemus* 6 (22) describes the arrival of Jesus in Hades. The legion of devils were stricken with terror, and Hades cried out: 'We are overcome! Woe unto us.'[3]

Finally, in the Ascension Jesus burst triumphantly through the demons who encircle the earth (Eph. 4.8), and so returned to glory.

No picture of Jesus is commoner in the thinking of the early Church than the picture of him as *Christus Victor*, the Conquering Christ. It may be that this is one of the pictures which is remote from us, but to a world haunted and hag-ridden by the thought of the demons there can have been nothing in this world so gloriously emancipating as the conviction that the power of the demons was broken. And even if in its particular expression this conception comes from a world of thought which is not our world, it still has this permanent truth that on the Cross a blow was struck which disarmed evil for ever. And it must be remembered that, however strange this idea is to western, civilized, sophisticated man, missionaries repeatedly tell us that for primitive peoples the greatest thrill that Christianity brings is the thrill of knowing that there is one loving God and not a world of hostile spirits and divinities.

[1] *Catechetical Lectures* 14.19.
[2] *Commentary On Romans* 5.1.
[3] M. R. James, *The Apocryphal New Testament,* p. 135.

(iv)   One of the great conceptions of the work of Jesus Christ, which runs through much of early Christian thought, and which is still dominant in the thought of the Greek Orthodox Church, is the idea of the deification of man because of what Jesus Christ has done. The whole idea is summed up in one great saying of Irenaeus, who spoke of the Word of God who, through his transcendent love, 'became what we are to make us what he is'.[1] The idea is that Jesus Christ by taking human nature upon himself freed human nature from the corruptibility which is the consequence of sin and deified it.

The scriptural warrant for any such conception comes from two New Testament passages. I Tim. 6.16 speaks of the Lord Jesus Christ 'who alone has immortality'. Immortality is in the gift of Jesus Christ. II Peter 1.4 tells how Christians through the work of Jesus Christ 'may escape from the corruption that is in the world because of passion, and become *partakers of the divine nature*'.

To us this is a startling idea. Two facts must be noted.

First, this conception does not mean that man becomes identical with God. Sometimes in Greek, when a noun is used without the definite article, it has a kind of adjectival force. To say that man could become *ho theos* would be to say that man can become identical with God, one and the same as God. But to say that a man can become *theos*— using the word without the definite article—is to say that a man can come to have the same kind of life and existence and being as God has, but without becoming identical with God. The conception of deification is that man through Jesus Christ can be lifted out of the life of fallen and corrupt humanity into the very life of God.

Second, startling as this idea may seem to us, it is part and parcel of ancient religious thought long before Christianity came into the world. Mrs Adam wrote: 'Through the course

[1]   *Against Heresies,* Preface to the fifth book, the last sentence.

of Greek religious thought a single thread may be traced,
the essential unity of man and God.'[1] Seneca writes: 'Why
should you not believe that something of divinity exists in
one who is a part of God (*dei pars*)?'[2] Aristotle declares that
virtue is achieved by man 'through something within him
that is divine'. 'We ought,' he says, 'as far as possible to
achieve immortality.'[3] Epictetus speaks of the true philos-
opher as a man 'who has set his heart on changing from a
man into a god', and such a man, even when he is in the
paltry body of death, has set his purpose 'upon fellowship
with Zeus'.[4] Plato talks of the goodness of man 'so long as
the inherited nature of God remained strong in him.'[5] He
says that when men fix their eyes on God, they are inspired,
and they receive from him their habits and their character
'in so far as it is possible for a man to have a part in God'.[6]
It was due to the gift of Prometheus that man became a
partaker of 'a divine portion', and so 'by the nearness of his
kin to God' man became the only creature who worships the
gods.[7] In *The Laws* he speaks of Lycurgus, the great Spartan
law-giver, as 'some man in whom human nature was blended
with the divine'.[8] Cicero says that knowledge of the gods
makes us 'in no way inferior to the celestials, except in
immortality'.[9] The Graeco-Roman world was well acquaint-
ed with the idea of the kinship of man and God.

This conception of unity with God came to its peak in
the pagan world in the experience of the devotees of the
Mystery Religions. The Mystery Religions were mainly
based on passion plays, exhibiting the sufferings, the death,
and the rising again of some god, played out under such
conditions of preparation and emotion that the initiate,
watching the play, experienced an actual union between him-

[1] *Greek Ideals of Righteousness,* p. 67.   [2] *Letters* 92.30.
[3] *Nicomachean Ethics* 10.7.8, 1177b 28,35.   [4] *Discourses*
2.19.27.   [5] *Critias* 120 D - 121 E.   [6] *Phaedrus* 230 A.
[7] Plato, *Protagoras* 322 A.   [8] *Laws* 691 E.   [9] *On the
Nature of the Gods* 2.61.

self and the god. 'I know thee, Hermes,' says the initiate, 'and thou knowest me. I am thou and thou art I.' 'Come to me, Lord Hermes,' he prayed, 'as babes to mother's wombs.'[1] When Christianity came into the world men were conditioned to accept and to understand the idea of deification in this sense.

In the early Church the conviction that Jesus Christ had done something tremendous to human nature by taking it upon himself was very common. Man by his sin had involved human nature in corruption and death; Jesus Christ by taking that human nature upon himself had reversed the process, and had lifted humanity into deity. Often the idea is that man by himself is neither mortal nor immortal but poised between the two, and in his union with Jesus Christ the potential of immortality is realized.

This belief in the deification of humanity through the work of Christ is most vividly and boldly expressed by the early Christian thinkers. 'By his passion,' said Irenaeus, 'the Lord destroyed death, dissipated error, rooted out corruption, destroyed ignorance, displayed life, showed truth, conferred incorruptibility.'[2] 'He was made man,' said Athanasius, 'that we might become God!'[3] 'The Son of God,' said Cyprian, 'suffered to make us sons of God.'[4] 'He was made a sharer in our mortality,' said Augustine. 'He made us sharers in his deity.'[5] Boldest of all is Clement of Alexandria, who was steeped in Greek thought. 'That man,' he writes, 'in whom the Logos dwells . . . that man becomes God, for God so wills it.'[6] 'The Logos of God became man that from man you might learn how man may become God.'[7] The Christian Gnostic, instructed by the Logos, is 'God walking about in the flesh'.[8]

---

[1] Samuel Angus, *The Mystery Religions and Christianity*, pp. 110f.   [2] *Against Heresies* 2.32.2.   [3] *On the Incarnation* 54.   [4] *Letters* 88.6.   [5] *On the Trinity* 4.8 2.4.   [6] *Paedagogus* 3.1.1.5.   [7] *Protrepticus* 1.8.4.   [8] *Stromateis* 7.16.101.4.

It is clearly to be noted that this process of the deification of human nature was never regarded as automatic. Origen held that it came from contemplation of God in Christ.[1] Frequently the idea is that it comes through the action of the sacraments. Ignatius called the bread of the Eucharist 'the medicine of immortality, the antidote that we should not die, but live for ever in Christ Jesus.'[2] According to Gregory of Nyssa baptism 'deifies the soul', and in the sacrament 'a healing seed is inserted into the body'.[3] A man had to accept Jesus Christ and all that Jesus Christ offers before this tremendous benefit should be his.

Once again we are moving here in a world of ideas which is strange to us. And yet in spite of the strangeness there remains the great, central, inescapable truth. The incarnation and the death and the resurrection of Jesus Christ, the coming of God into humanity, did something for human nature which cannot be undone. Call it deification, call it what we will, something has happened to manhood because godhead took manhood upon itself.

(v)   It may well be that of all the conceptions of the work which Jesus Christ wrought for men that which has been most influential is that of Jesus as the Victim and the Sacrifice for the sin of man. The idea of Jesus as the sacrificial victim for the sin of man may be said to take three forms.

(a)   There is the idea that the death of Jesus is the *ransom* price paid for the liberation of man from the bondage in which he was held, and from which he could never free himself.

There is real scriptural basis for this view. 'The Son of Man,' said Jesus, 'came not to be served but to serve, and to give his life as a ransom for many' (Matt. 20.28; Mark 10.45). 'There is one God and there is one mediator

---

[1]   *Commentary on John* 32.37.   [2]   *To the Ephesians* 20.2.
[3]   *Catechetical Oration* 33-37.

between God and man, the man Christ Jesus, who gave himself as a ransom for all' (I Tim. 2.5f.). 'You know,' wrote Peter, 'that you were ransomed from the futile ways inherited from your fathers, not with perishable things such as silver or gold, but with the precious blood of Christ' (I Peter 1.18f.).

There is a group of New Testament words connected with this picture. There is the word *lutron* (Matt. 20.28; Mark 10.45). In classical Greek it is usually used in the plural *lutra*, and it means 'the price paid for the emancipation or the liberation of any person or thing'. It is used in Homer for the price paid to ransom the body of Hector; it is regularly used in the papyri for the price paid for the freedom of a slave or for the redemption of something which is in pledge or pawn. In the Old Testament it is used of the price which a man must pay, if he is not to suffer the death penalty for something for which he is responsible (Ex. 21.30). It is used for the redemption of the first-born (Num. 3.12,46-49,51; 18.15). It is declared that there is no *lutron* for the life of a murderer (Num. 35.31), and it is used of the ransom price of captives taken in war (Isa. 45.13). Closely connected is the word *antilutron* (I Tim. 2.6). There is the word *lutrousthai* which means 'to ransom' or 'to redeem', to pay the price necessary for liberation. Jesus gave himself that he might *redeem* us from all iniquity (Titus 2.14; I Peter 1.18). There is the word *lutrōsis*, which means 'redemption'. Jesus obtained redemption for us by his own blood (Hebrews 9.12). Commonest of all there is the word *apolutrōsis*, which means 'the act of redeeming', or the 'redemption' won by such an act. We are put into a right relationship with God through the *redemption* that is in Jesus Christ (Romans 3.24). We have *redemption* through the blood of Jesus Christ (Eph. 1.14; 4.30; Col. 1.14; cp. Rom. 8.23; I Cor. 1.30; Heb. 9.15).

All these words describe the paying of the price which is

necessary to liberate a man from a bondage or from a situation from which he cannot in any circumstances liberate himself.

Closely connected with this picture and idea there are two other words, *agorazein* and *exagorazein*, which mean 'to buy', 'to purchase', 'to buy out from'. Christians have been *bought* with a price (I Cor. 6.20; 7.23). Christ has *redeemed* us, *bought us out from* the law and its curse (Gal. 3.13; 4.5). These words are specially appropriate for buying a slave out of his slavery into freedom.

There is abundant evidence in the New Testament for the idea of Jesus Christ as the ransom, and the redemption for the sin of man.

Certain things must be said about the interpretation of the work of Jesus Christ in terms of ransom.

First, as David Smith points out in *The Atonement in the Light of History and the Modern Spirit* (pp. 62-64), there can have been few more relevant pictures of the work of Christ, if that work was to be stated in terms contemporary with first-century life. This was the age of brigandage and piracy; the traveller travelled in danger; at any time he might be captured, and held to ransom, and a ransom had to be found, if his freedom was to be regained.

After the Battle of Adrianople in the fourth century, Ambrose, the great Bishop of Milan, spent his all to ransom the captives taken in battle. In the end he even melted down the sacred vessels of the sacrament and turned them into coinage, and, when he was accused of sacrilege, he answered that the souls for which the Lord's blood had been shed were surely more precious then the vessels which contained it.

'Remember them that are in bonds,' says the writer to the Hebrews (Heb. 13.3). It is one of the charges of Ignatius against the false teachers that 'for love they have no care, none for the widow, none for the orphan, none for the

distressed, none for the afflicted, *none for the prisoner*.[1]
Clement of Rome in his letter to Corinth prays: 'Save those
of us who are in affliction, have mercy on the lowly, raise
the fallen, show thyself to those in need, heal the sick, turn
again the wanderers of thy people, feed the hungry, ransom
the prisoners, raise up the weak, comfort the faint-hearted.'[2]
The prisoners awaiting ransom even found their way into
the liturgies. In the *Liturgy of St Mark* we read: 'Them that
are holden in prisons or in mines or in exile or bitter
bondage, pity them all, deliver them all.' The *Liturgy of
St James* includes the prayer: 'Remember, O Lord, Christians at sea, on the road, among strangers, those in mines
and tortures and bitter bondage, being our fathers and
brethren.' In the early days men knew all about the unhappy
captive and the need for ransom, for the captives and the
prisoners were in their hearts and in their prayers. Here was
a picture of the work of Jesus Christ which all men could
grasp and understand.

There was another ancient custom which would make the
picture of ransom meaningful to earliest Christian thought.
There was one way in which it was possible for a Greek
slave to gain his freedom. For many years he might save all
he could of the very little money which it was possible for
him to earn. As he saved the money, he could take it and
deposit it in the temple of some god. When after years of
saving he had amassed his own purchase price, he could
take his master to the temple where the money had been
deposited. There the money was handed over to the master
and the slave was free. But the idea behind this was that it
was *the god* who paid the purchase price; the god bought
the slave for himself to be his own. The slave, therefore,
became the property of the god, and so free from all human
ownership. This is not an analogy which can be overstressed

1   *To the Smyrnaeans* 6.2.
2   *I Clement* 59.4.

in its details, for it was the slave himself who scrimped and saved to collect his own purchase price, and, therefore, he was freed by the result of his own efforts; but the idea that the god had bought the slave for himself made men familiar with the divine purchase of a man that that man might be freed, liberated, emancipated from the slavery and the bondage in which he was held.

There is no doubt that in the early Church the idea of divine ransom would speak to men's hearts in terms which they knew and understood. There were few ways in which the work of Jesus Christ could be made more vividly real to men.

For the moment we will not discuss or criticize this picture. We must first set beside it, and consider with it, certain kindred and closely connected pictures.

(b) There is the idea that the death of Jesus is the *sacrifice* which atones for the sin of man. There are two general things to be said about this idea. First, it is the most universal of all ideas. However a man is going to express this, however he is going to work it out, however, to use a technical term, he is going to conceptualize this, he knows that this is in fact what actually happened in the life and the death of Jesus. Paul spoke of the Son of God who loved him and who gave himself for him (Gal. 2.20), and that is the simplest expression of Jesus as the supreme and availing sacrifice for all mankind. This is not so much one expression of what Jesus did; it is the essential, basic idea behind any possible expression of what Jesus did. Second, it would be next to impossible for a Jew to express his idea of the work of Jesus in any other way. Orthodox Jewish religion was founded on the sacrificial system. It was so founded because it was founded on the law. When God entered into the covenant relationship with Israel, in which he was to be their God and they were to be in a special sense his people, that relationship was founded on the law (Ex. 24.7). It is the dilemma of the human situation that man cannot perfectly keep the law. Were the matter left there, it would mean that the relationship between God and his people must be irretrievably broken. But there enters into the matter the whole sacrificial system, whose aim it is by penitence and by sacrifice to atone for breaches of the law, that is, for sin, and so to restore the broken relationship between God and his covenant people. In Jewish religion it was sacrifice which restored the lost and broken relationship between God and man. Jesus was supremely and uniquely the one who restored the lost relationship between God and man, whose work bridged the gulf which sin had created between God and man, who made it possible for the sinner to receive forgiveness and to enter into the presence of God. How else, then, was it possible for a Jew to express the work of Jesus? Jesus to the Jew must be the supreme sacrifice who brings together again man and God, when man and God were separated, and when man was under condemnation, because of sin.

God put forward Jesus as an expiation (*hilastērion*) by his blood, to be received by faith (Rom. 3.25). Christ our paschal lamb (*pascha*) has been sacrificed (I Cor. 5.7). He is the expiation for our sins (I John 2.2); God sent his Son to be the expiation for our sins (I John 4.10); in both cases the word is *hilasmos*. Here is the very basis of the Letter to the Hebrews. The function of the priest is to offer sacrifice, but the proof that such sacrifices are unavailing is the unanswerable fact that they have to be made over and over again every day in life; but Christ offered for all time a single sacrifice for sins (Heb. 10.11f.). It was not the blood of goats and calves he took, but his own blood, thus securing an eternal redemption (Heb. 9.12). He offered himself without blemish to God (Heb. 9.14).

Here is a picture which stands at the very centre of all Jewish religion, a picture of the work of Jesus to which the mind and the heart instinctively respond, and which the human spirit witnesses to be true. Once again we shall leave the discussion of it, until we have stated its kindred conceptions.

(c) We now turn to one of the most famous of all interpretations of the work of Jesus Christ, the interpretation which thinks of the work of Jesus in terms of *satisfaction*. It will be at once seen that there is no biblical basis at all for the terminology of this theory; it is expressed in terms and categories which are almost entirely non-biblical and which are the terms and categories of chivalry and knight-hood; for it was in the age of chivalry that this interpretation was born. The Satisfaction interpretation of the work of Jesus Christ was worked out by Anselm in his famous book *Cur Deus Homo* (*Why God became Man*), which he gave to the public in AD 1098.

Anselm begins by defining sin. Every living creature in the universe, angel and man alike, owes God perfect obedience to God's law. If that obedience were given, there would be no sin. Sin is failure to render to God what is owed to God, and that which is owed to God is perfect submission to his law and will. This is the one honour which is owed to God and which God desires. To fail to render this obedience to God is to take away from God what is his by right, and to 'put God out of his honour'. In an age of chivalry it was a first principle that he whose honour was belittled or injured must seek satisfaction, and so, says Anselm, it is with God.

But, even if God's honour is injured and insulted, why cannot God simply, by an act of grace and pardon and mercy, forgive? Why is satisfaction necessary? First, God is the moral governor of the universe, and, if his honour can be insulted with impunity and without due satisfaction being paid, then the moral government of the universe is weakened and discredited. To maintain the moral government of the universe, its moral governor must exact satisfaction when his law is broken and his honour insulted. Second, God demands of men that they should unconditionally forgive each other and that they should never exact vengeance. Why does he not do the same himself? The answer is that herein is precisely the difference between man and God. Vengeance belongs to God; man, because he is man, must unconditionally forgive; God, because he is God, has the right to act in vengeance.

The result of this is that man is confronted with an alternative from which there is no escape—satisfaction or punishment—there is no third way. How then can this satisfaction be found? The supreme human dilemma is that it cannot be found by man, for the simple reason that there is nothing which any man can ever do or be which he does not already owe to God. There is nothing *extra*, no work of supererogation which a man can offer to God. That is even true of penitence. If a man sins, penitence is no more than he owes, and satisfaction demands the extra thing. So, then, man is helpless, and in a situation in which he must be punished, because no satisfaction is possible.

It is here that Jesus enters upon the scene. He became man, and in man and for man he offers to God the complete obedience to the will of God and the complete submission to God which alone can satisfy the honour of God. Since Jesus does this in and for man, God can accept this satisfaction, and so can forgive and withhold punishment without compromising his moral authority and without lowering his divine dignity. The complete obedience of Jesus to the law and to the will of God is the offering which satisfies the injured honour of God, and which saves man from the penalty and punishment which his sin had necessitated. Whatever else may be true of Anselm's interpretation of the work of Jesus, this much is certainly true—in Anselm it is *the whole of Jesus* which is important. His work for man is not confined to his death; it extends over his whole life, and his death is simply the ultimate climax and consummation of this life of complete submission to God and perfect service and satisfaction of the honour of God. According to Anselm, Jesus did for man, in his life and death as man, what man could never have done for himself.

Once again there is no doubt that this picture and interpretation of the work of Jesus Christ would speak to the age in which it was first expressed and stated. It was the mediaeval age which thought and lived and acted in terms of knighthood and of chivalry, in which great and knightly tales were told of how honour was injured and honour was vindicated. Once again we shall leave the criticism and evaluation of it until we have examined the last of the great kindred views of the work of Jesus.

(d) There is the interpretation of the work of Jesus Christ for men in terms of *substitution*. Before we look at this idea in its wider aspect, we may look at it in its narrower aspect in what has been called its forensic form, which is a form which is specially connected with Reformation thought.

The basic idea behind this is that God is King, Law-giver and Judge. Sin is the breaking of God's law, and the consequence and result of sin is to leave man a criminal under judgment at God's judgment-seat. In such a position there is nothing for which man can look except utter condemnation and consequent punishment. The idea is that Jesus Christ offered himself as a substitute on our behalf and endured the punishment which should have fallen upon us. He is the substitute for sinners; he suffered in our stead. This is the conception which finds such an astonishing fore-shadowing in the picture of the Suffering Servant in Isa. 53: 'He was wounded for our transgressions, he was bruised for our iniquities; upon him was the chastisement which made us whole, and with his stripes we are healed. All we like sheep have gone astray; we have turned every one to his

own way; *and the Lord has laid on him the iniquity of us all'*
(Isa. 53.5f.). As David Smith sums up this idea: 'We lay, by
reason of our sin both original and actual, under the wrath
and curse of God, sentenced to an eternity of torment; and
the doom would have been executed upon us had not Christ
offered himself in our room and suffered in our stead the
stroke of God's wrath, and thus satisfied his justice and
appeased his anger.'[1]

David Smith illustrates this by the old children's hymn:

> He knew how wicked men had been
> He knew that God must punish sin;
> So out of pity Jesus said
> He'd bear the punishment instead,

and by Mrs Cousin's hymn:

> Jehovah lifted up his rod;
>   O Christ, it fell on thee!
> Thou wast sore stricken of thy God;
>   There's not one stroke for me.
>   Thy tears, thy blood,
>   Beneath it flowed;
>   Thy bruising healeth me.
>
> Jehovah bade his sword awake;
>   O Christ, it woke 'gainst thee!
> Thy blood the flaming blade must slake,
>   Thy heart its sheath must be.
>   All for my sake,
>   My peace to make:
>   Now sleeps that sword for me.

The substitutionary view of the work of Jesus holds
definitely and distinctly that Jesus Christ on his Cross bore
the penalty and the punishment for sin which we should have
borne, and that he did so as an act of voluntary and spontaneous and sacrificial love.

There is a sense in which this interpretation of the work
of Jesus has in modern times fallen into disrepute. It has
undergone much criticism, and there are many thinkers who

[1]   *The Atonement in the Light of History and the Modern Spirit,*
     p. 103.

have recoiled from it. But two things have to be said. First, there is the quite general truth that the heart of man witnesses that there is something here which is fundamentally true. John Oxenham has in one of his books an imaginary picture of Barabbas, after he had been set free. Something about Jesus had captured Barabbas and he followed him out to see the end. And, as Barabbas saw Jesus hang upon his Cross, one thought was beating into his mind: 'I should have been hanging there—not he—he saved me!' There is no doubt that that is the reaction of the heart to the Cross. We have only to remember how this idea has captured so many of the great evangelical hymns of the Church to see how it appeals to the human heart. It is there in Henry Williams Baker's hymn:

> In perfect love he dies;
>   For me he dies, for me!
> O all-atoning Sacrifice,
>   I cling by faith to thee.

It is there in Cecil Frances Alexander's hymn:

> There was no other good enough
>   To pay the price of sin;
> He only could unlock the gate
>   Of heaven, and let us in.

It is there in the hymn of Charles Wesley which has well-nigh become the magnificent anthem of Methodism:

> And can it be, that I should gain
>   An interest in my Saviour's blood?
> Died he for me, who caused him pain
>   For me who him to death pursued?
> Amazing love! how can it be
> That thou, my God, shouldst die for me?
>
> No condemnation now I dread;
>   Jesus, and all in him, is mine!
> Alive in him, my living Head,
>   And clothed in righteousness divine,
> Bold I approach the eternal throne,
> And claim the crown through Christ my own.

There is no doubt that the idea of Jesus Christ as the great willing substitute who bore the punishment which should have fallen on every sinful man is dear to the Christian heart.

The second general truth is this: this is an interpretation and understanding of the Cross which has existed without break since the beginning of Christian thought. In the New Testament itself we have Paul writing to the Corinthians that God 'made him to be sin who knew no sin, so that in him we might become the righteousness of God' (II Cor. 5.21). We can trace this picture down through patristic thought.

'Who,' said Tertullian, 'ever paid for the death of another by his own except the Son of God?' 'He had come for this purpose that he himself, free from all sin and altogether holy, should die for sinners.'[1] 'Christ,' said Cyprian, 'bore us all in that he bore our sins.'[2] 'The Son of God,' he says, 'did not disdain to take the flesh of man, and, although he was not a sinner, himself to carry the sins of others.'[3] 'God,' says Hilary, 'aims at the purchase of the salvation of the whole human race by the offering of this holy and perfect victim.'[4] 'He underwent death,' said Ambrose, 'to give satisfaction for those who were under judgment.'[5] 'If man had not sinned,' said Augustine, 'the Son of Man would not have come.'[6] There is no age in Christian thought to which the idea of Jesus Christ as the Saviour, whose death was voluntary, vicarious, sacrificial, substitutionary, has not been dear.

We have now seen the main great interpretations under which the work of Jesus Christ has been understood. How shall we evaluate them? Broadly speaking, they may be grouped under three classes.

(i)   There is the interpretation which thinks of the work of Jesus in terms of *ransom*. We have already seen how vivid

---

[1] *On Chastity* 22.   [2] *Letters* 62.13.   [3] *On the Goodness of Patience* 6.   [4] *Commentary on Psalm* 53.13.   [5] *Concerning Flight from the World* VII, 4.   [6] *Sermon* 174.2.

and meaningful that interpretation must have been to an age in which piracy and brigandage flourished and in which the need for ransom was often a bitter necessity, an age in which life was founded on slavery and in which emancipation was the dearest dream of millions of men and women. But immediately this interpretation is literalized, it runs headlong into one problem—*To whom was the ransom paid?*

There were those like Bernard of Clairvaux who insisted that the ransom was paid to the devil, who had men in his power. 'No one,' he says, 'seeks a Redeemer who does not know himself a captive.' He argues that the devil had power, and just power, over men. Because of man's sin, the devil's power over men was justly permitted by God. Certainly the devil's will and intention were not just but evil; but the fact that he had power over men was just, in that it was permitted by God. 'Man was justly given over, but mercifully delivered.' 'And there was not lacking a certain justice in the very deliverance, since this also concerned the Deliverer's mercy that he should rather employ justice against the assailant than power.'[1] Bernard did not see anything impossible in holding that the ransom was paid to the devil, for it was in the justice of God that man in his sin had fallen into the power of the devil, and it befitted God to deal with the devil also in justice.

But there were many more who could not possibly hold that the ransom was paid to the devil, for to conceive of God paying a ransom to the devil is to put the devil on a bargaining equality with God. So Origen writes: 'To whom did Christ give his soul for ransom? Surely not to God. Could it then be to the Evil One? For he had us in his power until the ransom for us should be given to him, even the life of Christ. The Evil One had been deceived and had been led to suppose that he was capable of mastering the soul (of

[1] Quoted in David Smith, *The Atonement in the Light of History and the Modern Spirit*, pp. 72,78,79.

Christ) and did not see that to hold him involved a trial of strength greater than he could successfully undertake.'[1] Here the idea is that in the soul of Christ the devil *thought* that he was receiving the ransom for sinning men, but in actual fact he did not know that he was receiving something which he was quite powerless to hold, and that in the attempt to hold it his power would be broken for ever. So in the same passage Origen goes on: 'Therefore death, though he thought that he had prevailed against him (that is, against Christ), no longer prevails against him, Christ then having become free among the dead and stronger than the power of death and so much stronger than death, that all who will among those who are mastered by death may follow him, death no longer prevailing against him. For everyone who is with Jesus is stronger than death.' Here then the idea is that in the soul of Christ the devil received what he thought was a ransom but what in the end was his destruction.

As time went on, this idea was elaborated, and the elaboration took the line that the Incarnation was a trick or stratagem played on the devil by God. The devil was tricked into thinking that he could master and control the soul of Christ, and in seeking to do so was finally defeated. More than once this was expressed in an almost grotesque metaphor. The human flesh of Christ was said to be the bait which was dangled before the devil; but the deity of Christ was the hook concealed within the bait. So the devil swallowed the bait and was caught by the hook, and his power was destroyed. Gregory of Nyssa says: 'The Deity was hidden under the veil of our nature, that, as is done by greedy fish, the hook of Deity might be gulped down along with the bait of the flesh, and thus, life being introduced into the house of death, and light shining in the darkness, that which is contradictory to light and life might vanish away; for it is not in the nature of darkness to remain where

[1] *Commentary on Matthew* 16.8.

light is present or of death to exist where life is present.'[1]
This idea of a trick played on the devil reaches its last
word in fantastic grotesqueness in the saying of Peter the
Lombard: 'The Cross was a mousetrap (*muscipula*) baited
with the blood of Christ.'[2]

So long as the idea of ransom remains a metaphor and a
picture, it has real and dramatic value. Whenever the
attempt is made to literalize it and to make it a theology, it
will not stand the test.

(ii)   The method of interpreting the work of Jesus in
terms of satisfaction has, as we have already noted, one
outstanding value. It gives a very real place to the life of
Christ in the work of Christ. It is the obedience of the whole
life of Christ and finally of the death of Christ which con-
stitutes that which satisfies the honour of God. But the one
insuperable fault in this interpretation is that it regards God
as the Moral Governor of the world. And so, of course, he is;
but to make the fact that God is the moral governor of the
world the one dominating and deciding factor in the whole
understanding of the work of Christ is to set out with a view
of God which is utterly inadequate. A moral governor's
honour may be insulted and injured; but that is strangely
different from the breaking of a father's heart.

(iii)   When we come to the interpretations of the work of
Jesus in terms of sacrifice and of substitution and of vicarious
suffering for us, we dare not treat them lightly; still less can
we dismiss them contemptuously as is sometimes done.
These interpretations must be regarded with real reverence,
because it is through them that a great host of people in
every age and generation have found peace for their hearts
and salvation for their souls. These ideas have always formed
the core and essence of evangelical preaching, and in every
generation they have been the moving power of conversion.

---

[1] *Catechetical Oration* 17 - 23.   [2] *Sentences* 2.19.

Nonetheless they have great and grave difficulties when they are pressed too far.

In the ransom interpretation of the work of Jesus, the ransom is offered in some sense to the devil; in the sacrifice and substitution interpretations of the work of Jesus the sacrifice is offered to God. The difficulty here is that in some sense God and Jesus are opposed. God demands sacrifice; Jesus gives sacrifice. The result of this is that almost inevitably Jesus is seen in terms of *love*, and God is seen in terms of *justice*. That is why a great many people who have been brought up on these interpretations either consciously or unconsciously love Jesus but fear God, and feel at home with Jesus but estranged and remote from God. These interpretations have the effect of setting God and Jesus over against each other.

We may put this in another way—and this is the most serious effect of literalizing the sacrifice and substitution interpretations of the work of Jesus. If we think in terms of sacrifice or in terms of substitution, it almost necessarily means that something that Jesus did changed the attitude of God to men, that before the action of Jesus God could only punish and condemn men and that after the action of Jesus God was able and willing to forgive men. If we think in terms of sacrifice, it means that Jesus offered a sacrifice which made it possible somehow for God to forgive men. If we think in terms of substitution, it means that man was the criminal at the judgment seat of God, and through the action of Jesus God's sentence of condemnation was changed into a verdict of acquittal.

There can be no doubt that that is a view which finds no support in Scripture. Nowhere does the New Testament speak of God being reconciled to men; always it speaks of men being reconciled to God. 'We beseech you,' says Paul, 'on behalf of Christ, be reconciled to God' (II Cor. 5.20). It was never the attitude of God to man which had to be changed; it was the attitude of man to God. Still further, the New Testament makes it quite clear that the whole process of salvation finds its initiative in the love of God. It was because God so loved the world that he sent his Son (John 3.16). It is his love for men that God shows in the work which Jesus performed (Rom. 5.8). 'In this is love,' says John, 'not that we loved God, but that he loved us and sent his Son to be the expiation for our sins' (I John 4.10). If one thing is clear, it is that there was no necessity to change the attitude of God to men. That attitude was always love.

An attempt to evade this difficulty is to argue, as Denney did, that it is never right to isolate one attribute of God. It is, therefore, necessary to remember that God is justice *and* love. It is then possible to go on to say that God's justice necessitates the punishment of sin and God's love equally necessitates the forgiveness of sin, and that, therefore, God in his love pays in Jesus Christ the penalty which his justice demands. The hymn would then be right to say of the Cross:

> O trysting-place where heaven's love
> And heaven's justice meet!

We can only speak with hesitating reverence, but it does seem that that view, however logically and neatly and theologically it seems to solve the problem, leaves God for ever a split personality in whom there is eternal tension between justice and love. The work of Christ on this basis would be as much a thing which solved the problem of God as a thing which wrought the salvation of man.

The great problem of all interpretations of the Cross in terms of sacrifice—in the Jewish sense of the term—and in terms of substitution is that they tend to set Jesus in opposition to God, and they must go on to say that something Jesus did in his life, and especially in his death, changed the attitude of God to men, or made it possible for God to treat men in a different way. When they are stated in their crudest way, when the implication is that God laid on Jesus Christ the punishment which should have been laid upon men in order that the divine justice might be maintained, then these interpretations do something even worse. They represent God as protecting his justice by the most monstrous act of injustice the universe has ever seen or ever can see; for he laid on the sinless one the punishment of sin. Even if it be argued that the acceptance by Christ of that situation was absolutely and completely voluntary and spontaneous, the terrible injustice remains.

If then none of the interpretations of the work of Jesus which we have so far examined are such that we can wholly and unreservedly accept them, even if we humbly recognize that which is precious in them and that which they have wrought in the minds and in the hearts and in the lives of men, where are we to turn?

In our examination of the various interpretations of the work of Jesus we omitted one. We omitted that which is attached to the name of Abelard who was born in 1079 and who died in 1142. J. K. Mozley briefly summarizes the teaching of Abelard: 'Christ died, neither because a ransom had to be paid to the Devil, nor because the blood of an innocent victim was needed to appease the wrath of God, but that a supreme exhibition of love might kindle a corresponding love in men's hearts and inspire them with the true freedom of sonship of God.'[1] This is sometimes called the *moral influence* interpretation of the work of Christ, although Mozley would say that its influence is as much emotional as it is moral.

Abelard had certain basic convictions. He refused to accept any interpretation of Jesus Christ's life and work, and especially of his death, which is based on the idea of ransom. Ransom to the Devil is unthinkable, ransom to God

[1] *The Doctrine of the Atonement*, p. 132.

is unnecessary. He based everything on the love of God. The Incarnation of Jesus Christ and the death of Jesus Christ are acts of pure love. Certainly God is righteous, but his righteousness is subordinate to his love, or, even more, his righteousness is his love. The problem, as Abelard saw it, is that sin has separated man from God, and the supreme necessity is to bring man back into a relationship of love and trust to God. There is no necessity for Christ to assuage the wrath of God, because God's attitude to man is not wrath but love. In order to win men back to this relationship to God, Jesus Christ has given to men the highest and the most unanswerable proof of love, a proof of love and an exhibition of love which so moves the hearts of men that they are enabled to enter into the relationship of love with God. The death of Christ on the Cross is not an objective transaction; it is rather the supreme *evidence* of that love which is demonstrated in the life of Christ from the beginning. This love calls forth love, so that we come to love him because he first loved us (I John 4.19, AV).

Abelard did not quite stop there. He went on to say that when this love is awakened in our hearts, God forgives us and reckons the merit of Christ to us, in that Christ is the head of the new humanity which begins in him. But the merit of Jesus does not lie in any accumulation of deeds which he did; the merit of Jesus is his obedience to God, and his service of God and men in utter love.[1] Abelard also believed that this loving ministry of Christ still goes on in that, as the writer to the Hebrews says, he always lives to make intercession for us (Heb. 7.25).

There is no doubt that there is much that is missing in Abelard's interpretation of the work of Christ, but Harnack

[1] Abelard's views are set out in his own works, the *Commentary on the Epistle to the Romans* and the *Christian Theology* 4 (Migne, *PL* 178, 1278f.). Abelard's position is very fairly stated in A. Harnack, *History of Dogma VI*, pp. 78-80.

is right, when, after making all the necessary criticisms, he says: 'Abelard had too keen a sense of the love of his God, and of the oneness of God and Christ, to entertain the Gnostic thought that God needs a sacrifice or an equivalent, or that for God Christ's death is a benefit.' To put Abelard's position very simply, we may say that he believed that Jesus Christ came to proclaim, to demonstrate and to exhibit the love of God, to say in his life and his death for men, 'God loves you like that.' He came to tell men that they are sinners, but they are already forgiven sinners, if only they will turn to God in response to the love of God. It was Abelard's view that Jesus Christ did nothing to alter the attitude of God, but that he came to tell men in speech and in action, in his life and in his death, what the attitude of God is to men. He came because, as Abelard believed, men had only to see the attitude of God to them, men had only to behold the love of God, to answer and to respond to it.

Let us now leave these interpretations of the work of Christ, and turn from his words about giving his life as a ransom to his other great words about his own death. We find these words in the account of the Last Supper. Jesus said of the bread: 'This is my body.' He said of the wine: 'This is my blood of the covenant, which is poured out for many for the forgiveness of sins' (Matt. 26.26-28; Mark 14.22-24). Or, as Paul gives us the words: 'This cup is the new covenant in my blood' (I Cor. 11.25).

What, then, is a *covenant*? A covenant is a special relationship entered into between two people. When God is one of the parties in the covenant relationship, there is a vital difference between such a covenant and a bargain or treaty or agreement in the ordinary sense of the term. In any ordinary agreement the two parties enter into it on level and on equal terms; but in the covenant relationship between God and man the whole initiative is with God; it is in his grace and mercy that he makes this approach to man, and man can only accept or refuse the offer of God. So, then, in the biblical use of the term a covenant is a relationship between God and men.

We read the story of the initiation of the first covenant relationship between God and the nation of Israel in Ex. 24.1-8. That original covenant was entirely dependent on the keeping of the law (Ex. 24.7). So long as Israel kept the law, the covenant relationship remained; when Israel broke the law the covenant relationship was interrupted, broken and destroyed. It was to meet that situation that the whole sacrificial system was designed and intended. A man broke the law; and a sacrifice offered in penitence and contrition was the means whereby the broken covenant relationship, either between an individual or between the nation and God, was restored. The covenant, then, is a special relationship between God and man, entered into solely on the gracious initiative of God, dependent on the keeping of the law of the covenant, and maintained by the institution of sacrifice with penitence, which restored the relationship when it had been broken by rebellion or disobedience.

But already in the Old Testament there are glimpses of a new covenant. Jeremiah heard God say that he would make a new covenant with the people, not like the covenant that he had once made with their fathers. This would be a covenant, not established by an externally imposed law, but written on their hearts and in their inward parts. It would be a covenant in which all men really and truly knew God. 'I will forgive their iniquity,' God said, 'and I will remember their sin no more' (Jer. 31.31-35). Two things stand out about this new covenant; it is a covenant based not on law but on the inward devotion of the heart, and there is no mention of sacrifice at all.

Two things are to be noted in the words of Jesus, as Paul relates them—'This cup is the new covenant in my blood' (I Cor. 11.25). Jeremiah also speaks of the *new* covenant

(Jer. 31.31; LXX 38.31). Both in Paul and in the Greek of Jeremiah the word for 'new' is *kainos*. Greek has two words for 'new'. There is *neos*, which is new only in point of time; a thing which is *neos* may simply be the most recent example or specimen of something which has for long existed and which has for long been produced. But *kainos* means not only new in point of time, but also *new in point of kind or quality*. With a thing which is *kainos* a new quality has entered into life and the world. Since that is so, a *new* (*kainos*) covenant is not simply an old covenant which has been renewed or restated; it is a covenant of a new and different kind. Second, Jesus says of this new covenant that it is *in* his blood. The Greek word for *in* is *en*; *en* can and does translate the Hebrew word *bᵉ*, which means *at the price of*. It may, therefore, well be that Jesus said that this new and different kind of covenant is made possible only at the cost and at the price of his blood. When we put this together, we see that Jesus said that a new relationship between man and God has become possible through his blood, that is, through his life and his death.

Here, then, we come to the crux and essence of the matter. We have seen that Jesus said that he came to give his life a ransom for many; but we have also seen that that cannot be taken with crude literalness, for, when we ask to whom the ransom was paid, it does not make sense to say that it was paid either to the devil or to God. We have seen that the whole initiative of redemption is in the love of God, and that there can be no question of placating an angry and a hostile God. And yet the fact remains that it is at the cost and price of the life and death of Jesus that this new relationship between man and God, foreshadowed by Jeremiah, alone can come into being. We have further seen that the new covenant foretold by Jeremiah is based neither on law nor on sacrifice, but only on love and on the devotion of the heart.

What, then, was Jesus doing in his life and in his death? The answer must be that in his life and in his death Jesus was demonstrating to men the eternal, unchangeable, unconquerable love of God. He was demonstrating to men that God is the Father who loves undefeatably and whose one desire is that the lost son should come home. When Jesus entered the world, when he healed the sick, comforted the sad, fed the hungry, forgave his enemies, he was saying to men: 'God loves you like that.' When he died upon the cross, he was saying: 'Nothing that men can ever do to God will stop God loving them. There is no limit to the love of God. There is no end beyond which that love will not go. God loves you like that.' That is why nothing less than death on the Cross would do. If Jesus had refused or escaped the Cross, if he had not died, it would have meant that there was some point in suffering and sorrow at which the love of God stopped, that there was some point beyond which forgiveness was impossible. But the Cross is God saying in Jesus: 'There is no limit to which my love will not go and no sin which my love cannot forgive.'

The work of Christ is not something *about which* a man must know; it is something which he must experience in his own heart and mind and life. It is not so much to be understood as it is to be appropriated. For that reason it is not enough to know how others have interpreted it. It is quite true that it would be arrogant and presumptuous folly completely to disregard the great classical interpretations of it; but nevertheless each man must interpret it for himself. But it can only be interpreted from the inside. In the preface to his *Cur Deus Homo*, Anselm said: 'Some men seek for reasons because they do not believe; we seek for them because we do believe.' Any consideration of the work of Christ must be not so much argument as witness. How then are we to interpret it for ourselves?

One thing I know—that because of Jesus Christ and because of what he is and did and does my whole relationship to God is changed. Because of Jesus Christ I know that God is my father and friend. Daily and hourly I experience the fact that I can enter into his presence with confidence and with boldness. He is no longer my enemy; he is no longer even my judge; there is no longer any unbridgeable gulf between him and me; I am more at home with God than I am with any human being in the human world. And all this is so because of Jesus Christ, and it could not possibly have happened without him. But how am I to express this in some kind of personal interpretation of the work of Jesus? We may begin with two general principles.

(i)   It is quite wrong to think that one must confine oneself to one of the great classical interpretations and to hold that it expresses the whole truth, to believe that it alone is right and that all the others are wrong, to believe that belief in any one of them is essential for salvation, and to hold that he who believes in any of the others is a heretic and unsaved.

There is a perfect demonstration of this in Nels Ferré's book *Know your Faith*. In one chapter of that book Nels Ferré thinks about the work of Christ and in the compass of three pages (pp. 57-59) he says the following things. 'The Son of God as Son of Man has met sin, law, and death head on and conquered them all. God has assumed our plight, the whole plight, in Jesus Christ, and come off victorious within genuine humanity.' Here is the statement of *Christ the Victor*. 'God as man assumed the burden of our sins that we might know who he is, who we are, and for what he has made us.' Here is Christ *the Sacrifice, the Substitute, the Victim*. 'He shared our whole human experience, becoming the summary and summit of man's history.' Here is the conception of *Recapitulation*. 'The Godman helps us to become Godmen. Paul prays not in vain that we all be filled with the fullness of God.' Here is the conception of *Deification*. 'We are bid to take Jesus Christ as our actual example, "to walk even as he walked", to be perfect even as God is perfect, yes, even to imitate God himself.' Here is the conception of Jesus Christ the perfect *Example*. Within the narrow compass of a few pages this great Christian theologian and man of God has used all the great classical interpretations of Jesus Christ. This is entirely as it should be. Herbert Kelly, founder of Kelham, and one of the great ecumenical influences of our time, once said: 'Is not the cause of all our weakness that what God meant as complementary, men have regarded as antithetical?'[1] The great classical interpretations of the work of Jesus are not antithetical, they are complementary, and to make anyone of them a slogan and a test of orthodoxy is profoundly wrong.

(ii)   In the evaluation of any interpretation of the work of Jesus we must not test it by the bringing to it of proof texts; we must bring it to, and bring to it, the whole of Scripture. We must test it not by any individual text, however central, but by the whole conception of God which meets us in Jesus Christ. That which divides us perhaps more than anything else is the attempt to erect whole theologies on single texts rather than on the total message of Jesus Christ. Luther dealt with the canon of Scripture with sovereign freedom. His way of accepting some books of the Bible and rejecting others would have branded him as one of the most radical of critics, had he been writing today, and involved him in no little argument in his own day. In regard to this he wrote: 'If, in the debates in which exegesis brings no decisive victories, our adversaries press the letter against Christ, we shall insist on Christ against the letter.'[2] The test of any interpretation is harmony or disharmony with the conception of God which

[1]   *No Pious Person*, ed. George Every, p. 117.
[2]   Quoted in E. Reuss, *History of the Canon of the Holy Scriptures in the Christian Church*, p. 332.

Jesus Christ brought to men. Anything that is unworthy of the God who is the God and Father of our Lord Jesus Christ must be unhesitatingly rejected.

When we bear all this in mind, we can lay it down that there are four great truths which we can affirm about the work of Jesus Christ.

(i)   *The work of Christ was a fourfold demonstration.* In Jesus Christ we see *God in his attitude to men.* A word is the expression of a thought and to say that Jesus is the Word of God (John 1.14) is to say that Jesus is the expression of the thought of God. This Jesus who fed the hungry and healed the sick and comforted the sorrowing and was the friend of outcasts and sinners is the expression of the attitude of God to men. The one basic truth with which all Christian thought about God must start out is that God is like Jesus. In Jesus Christ we see *what man ought to be.* Jesus is not, as it were, *less* human than men, he is *more* human than men. In him there is the demonstration of what God intended man to be. In Jesus Christ we see *the perfect demonstration of the love of God.* As we see Jesus in his tenderness to the suffering and the sinning and the sorrowing, we can say: 'God loves me like that.' As we see Jesus on the Cross, we can say: 'God loves me enough to do that for me.' In the events which happened to Jesus Christ we see *the demonstration of the awfulness of sin.* In the death of Jesus Christ we see the wicked hands of men taking and destroying the loveliest life the universe has ever seen, or ever will see. On the Cross we see the terrible destructive power of sin, as it has been called, 'the infinite damnability of sin'. The effect of this must be to impel men to love God and to hate sin and to adore Jesus Christ. In this Abelard is profoundly right; unquestionably there is truth in the Moral Influence interpretation of the work of Jesus Christ, even if it is not the whole truth, and, even if a man never got past that interpretation he would have gone a long way, for he would inevitably be lost in wonder, love, and praise.

(ii) *The work of Christ is sacrificial work*. But that sacrifice was not offered to the devil, for the devil can never be on an equality with God; nor was that sacrifice offered to God, for nothing was ever needed to change the attitude of God to men, or to reconcile God to men. The whole process of which Jesus Christ is the centre and soul begins in the love of God. Wherein then does the sacrifice lie? It lies in this—*it cost the life and the death of Jesus Christ to tell men what God is like*. Without the life and death of Jesus Christ men could never have known what God is like, and could therefore never have entered into a loving relationship with God. It took all that Jesus Christ had to give to enable men to enter into this relationship with God. Only through Jesus Christ can I ever know that God loves me, not because of what I am, but because of what he is.

That sacrifice begins with the Incarnation. He who was rich for our sakes became poor (II Cor. 8.9). It culminates upon the Cross, for Jesus, having loved his own, loved them to the end (John 13.1). But why the death of Christ? The death of Christ was necessary for this reason—if Jesus in his love had stopped short of the Cross, it would have meant that there was somewhere beyond which the love of God would not go, that there was something beyond which God would not forgive. On the Cross God says to us in Jesus Christ: 'Nothing—absolutely nothing that you can do—can stop me loving you.' The Cross is the essential fact in the whole work of Christ.

No interpretation of the work of Christ even begins to be adequate unless it remembers the terrible sacrifice it cost to enable men to see the love of God that they might respond to it. The sacrifice which is in the work of Christ is neither sacrifice to the devil nor sacrifice to God. It is sacrifice *by* God necessitated by his great and gracious act of self-revelation in Jesus Christ.

(iii)   *The work of Christ is objective in its character.* It is objective in the sense that it quite definitely produces and achieves something which for ever continues to exist. It is not objective in the sense in which a legal transaction is objective. It is objective in this sense—it produced a completely new situation in regard to the relationship between God and man. It produced a situation which had not existed before, and which, once it had been produced, cannot cease to exist. It produced a situation in which there became possible between man and God a new relationship of intimacy, of confidence, of trust, of love. Prior to the work of Jesus Christ men did not fully know what God was like; between man and God there was the great gulf of ignorance or of semi-knowledge. The power of God, the justice of God, the holiness of God, the righteousness of God, men did know, but of the marvel of the love of God they had never dreamed. Men like Hosea glimpsed it, but in Christ it was fully and for ever displayed. The objective effect of the work of Jesus Christ is to create a new relationship between God and man, not by changing the attitude of God to man, but by revealing to men what the attitude of God to them is.

(iv)   *The work of Christ is effective in its dealing with sin.* There are certain things in this connection about which we must be clear. The work of Christ is not to be confined to his death, but necessarily includes that which comes to man through his life and his resurrection. At its lowest and its most obvious, the work of Christ provides man with the example of the good life. He left us an example that we should follow in his steps (I Peter 2.21). But the work of Christ goes far beyond that, or it would be quite unavailing for the helplessness of man. A fine example can be the most daunting and depressing thing in the world, if all it does is to convince a man of the impossibility of following it. Man does not need only *example*, he also needs *power*. Further, the work of Christ does not deal with sin in the sense of wiping out the consequences of sin. To be forgiven does not mean to be freed from the consequences of sin. If a man sins against his body, he will bear the consequences in his body, even when he is forgiven. If a man's sinning damages himself or other people, as it must, forgiveness does not remove the damage that he has done.

It is here that the Resurrection must come in. 'If,' says Paul, 'while we were enemies we were reconciled to God by the death of his Son, much more, now that we are reconciled, shall we be saved by his life' (Rom. 5.10). We are not dependent on a Christ who lived and died, we are dependent on a Christ who lived and died and who is alive for evermore. Since he is alive, he is here in such a way that we can draw upon him for power other than our own.

The work of Christ, therefore, enables us to deal effectively through him with the situations in which sin had rendered us helpless. It enables us to deal with the situation which sin had created *between a man and himself*. A man remains a split personality, poised between goodness and badness, between right and wrong, between heroism and cowardice, between sainthood and sin, between the ape and the angel, until the power of the Risen Christ takes possession of him, and makes him a personality integrated by this new centre within it. 'It is no longer I who live,' said Paul, 'but Christ who lives in me; and the life I now live in the flesh I live by faith in the Son of God, who loved me and gave himself for me' (Gal. 2.20). Through the work of Christ a man ceases to be a battle-ground of opposing forces and reaches mature manhood (Eph. 4.13). It enables us to deal with the situation which sin had created *between us and our fellowmen*. One of the great effects of sin is the disturbance of personal relationships; one of the great effects of the work of Christ is the creation of fellowship. It is only in Christ that men can find unity instead of disunity, trust instead of suspicion, love instead of hate. The mutual hostility which is created by sin is defeated by the love which is shed abroad by Christ. It enables us to deal with the situation which sin had created *between us and God*. The work of Christ assures us of the love and of the forgiveness of God, and our desire to hide from God is changed into a great desire to live for ever with God.

The work of Christ is effective, first, in revealing to us the love of God, and, second, in enabling us by his risen power to deal with the tragic and disastrous situations which sin has created in our own lives and in the life of the world.

No man can ever grasp, still less express, all that Jesus Christ has done, but we may be well content to witness with all our hearts that through Jesus Christ we have entered into a relationship with God, which without him would have been utterly impossible, and in him we have entered into a relationship with ourselves and with our fellowmen in which the deadly work of sin can be undone.

11

THE RESURRECTION

IT was not long after three o'clock in the afternoon when Jesus died (Mark 15.34). The next day was the Sabbath, and the Sabbath began at 6 p.m. According to the Jewish law a criminal's body might not remain on its cross over the Sabbath day, and therefore the body of Jesus had to be quickly taken down and quickly disposed of. Very often the bodies of crucified criminals were simply left to be the prey of the vultures, the carrion crows, and the pariah dogs. But the followers of Jesus had an influential friend who was able to help them to pay what they thought was their last tribute to their dead Master. His name was Joseph of Arimathaea; he was rich and devout; he was a member of the Sanhedrin, and in secret he was a disciple of Jesus. He went to Pilate and requested the body of Jesus that he might give it decent burial. Pilate was surprised that Jesus had died so soon, but was willing to accede to the request. The tombs of wealthy families in those days were not graves in the ground, but were caves with shelves on which the bodies were laid. Joseph had such a tomb, never hitherto used, in a garden near to Calvary. Nicodemus, John says, came with a gift of spices to embalm the body of Jesus as if it had been the body of a king. So the body of Jesus was wrapped in the grave-clothes, which were like long linen bandages wound round and round the body, and then it was laid on one of the shelves of the rock tomb. Such tombs were not closed with a door, but with a great circular stone like a cartwheel which ran in a groove and which was wheeled up to close the opening. So Jesus was laid in the tomb and the great stone, which one New Testament manuscript, Codex Bezae, says that twenty men could hardly have moved, was rolled up in its groove to close the tomb (Matt. 27.57-60; Mark 15.42-46; Luke 23.50-55; John 19.38-42). And the women who had been there at the foot of the cross marked the place where the body of Jesus was laid (Matt. 27.61; Mark 15.47).

Meanwhile the Jewish authorities had not been idle. Even after they had seen Jesus die on the cross they were still uneasy about him. They went to Pilate and asked that special precautions should be taken, lest the disciples of Jesus should steal his body and claim that he had risen from the dead. Pilate agreed that a guard should be posted and that the stone should be sealed to make things as safe as they could be made (Matt. 27.62-66). The time was to come when the bewildered guards had to report that the tomb was empty, and when they were bribed by the Jewish authorities to say that Jesus' disciples had stolen his body (Matt. 28.11-14).

All the Sabbath day, our Saturday, the body of Jesus lay in the tomb, and the tomb had no visitor, for the Sabbath day was the day of rest, and to have made even the journey from the city to the tomb would have been to break the Sabbath law. Then there came the first day of the week, our Sunday, the first Easter Sunday. It is little wonder that we cannot construct an hour-to-hour time-table of what happened on that day, for its events were so staggering that those who were involved in them must have for ever looked back on them with a kind of incredulous amazement. We can only reconstruct the story as well as we are able.

With the first streaks of dawn, even when it was still dark, the women came to the tomb to give to the body of Jesus their last loving service. There was Mary Magdalene, there was Mary the mother of James and Joses, there was Joanna, and maybe there were others. They were worried about the problem of gaining an entry to the tomb, and could not think how they might be able to move the massive stone which guarded its entrance. But, when they reached the tomb, the stone was rolled away, and there was a messenger to tell them that Jesus was risen and had gone before them into Galilee as he had promised that he would do (Matt. 28.1-7; Mark 16.1-8; Luke 24.1-11). As Matthew has it, the risen Jesus himself appeared to them on their way back to the city, and himself repeated the message of the messenger (Matt. 28.8-10).

It would be only natural that the women would rush with the news to the other disciples. Luke tells us that the rest of the disciples flatly refused to believe the news (Luke 24.10f.). But John goes on to tell us more. As he tells the story, Mary Magdalene hurried to tell the story of the empty tomb to Peter and to the disciple whom Jesus loved, but at that time she had not grasped the significance of the empty tomb, but was heart-broken because she thought that someone had taken away the body of Jesus. Peter and the beloved disciple set out for the garden. The beloved disciple saw the empty tomb and the grave-clothes lying in it, but he did not go into it. Then Peter came and went in. 'He saw the linen cloths lying, and the napkin, which had been on his head, not lying with the linen cloths but rolled up in a place by itself.' Then the other disciple also entered the tomb and saw and believed (John 20.6-8). What was it about the grave-clothes and the napkin that was so impressive? There are two possibilities. It may be that the grave-clothes and the napkin were so neatly and tidily laid out and folded that it was quite clear that there had been no hurried theft of the body, but that they had been carefully taken off and laid away. It is just possible that the Greek could mean that the linen grave-clothes and the head-napkin were lying separately, exactly as if the body of Jesus had evaporated out of them and left them lying empty there. So Peter and the beloved disciple returned to Jerusalem with the dawning certainty that Jesus had risen from the dead.

As John tells the story, it is clear that Mary Magdalene did not know what was going on. She lingered sorrowfully in the garden, until, in what some one has called the greatest recognition scene in literature, she suddenly recognized Jesus.

There followed on the same day the special appearance of the risen Jesus to Peter (Luke 24.34; cp. Mark 16.7), and what must have been the scene of reconciliation between Jesus and the disciple who loved him but denied him? There followed still on the same day the appearance of Jesus to the two friends who were walking the road to Emmaus (Luke 24.13-35).

There were still other appearances of Jesus. He appeared to his disciples apparently in the upper room, once when Thomas was absent and refused to believe, and once when Thomas came back to express his worship and his adoration (Luke 24.44-49; John 20.24-29).

These were all appearances in Jerusalem; but Matthew has the story of the appearance of Jesus to his disciples on the hill-top in Galilee and of his commission to them to go to preach the gospel (Matt. 28.16-20), and John tells of the appearance to the disciples as they were fishing on the sea-shore of the Sea of Galilee (John 21).

Such, then, is the account of the Resurrection as it appears in the New Testament itself, and it is on this account that the microscope of criticism has been turned; and there is an astonishing diversity in the results. Lives of Jesus such as F. W. Farrar's *Life of Christ* and David Smith's *In the Days of His Flesh* do little more than repeat the New Testament account with placid acceptance. But it is a very different story when we come to the work of the more modern and the more radical New Testament scholars. To read such works as C. Guignebert's *Jesus* (pp. 490-536), M. Goguel's *Jesus the Nazarene* (pp. 216-241), O. Holtzmann's *Life of Jesus* (pp. 492-529), J. Klausner's *Jesus of Nazareth* (pp. 356-359), C. G. Montefiore's *Synoptic Gospels* (I, 397-400), K. Lake's *The Historical Evidence for the Resurrection of Jesus*, J. Weiss's *Earliest Christianity* (I, 14-31, Harper's Torchbooks Edition), is to see how little radical criticism leaves of the New Testament story. And, if we go further back, we will find the work of Strauss and Renan equally devastating. It is necessary that we should at least be aware of the radical attack, for many of its claims and positions have, as it were, vaguely filtered down into popular knowledge, and it is sometimes forgotten that there remains not a little to be said on the other side as, for instance, in A. M. Ramsey's *The Resurrection of Christ*, or, more popularly, in James Martin's *Did Jesus Rise from the Dead?* Let us then see the lines which radical criticism has taken.

In the main it may be said that radical criticism has denied, or cast doubt upon, three facts or sets of facts. It denies the fact of the empty tomb; it denies the Jerusalem appearances of Jesus; it denies the objectivity of these appearances in any real sense of the term. The length to which this denial has gone may be seen from the last sentence of Guignebert's examination of the Resurrection narratives and of the Easter faith. He talks about the centrality of the belief in the Resurrection, but he concludes by saying: 'It is doubtful, however, whether the dogma of the Resurrection, which has so long been the mainstay of Christianity, has not, in our day, become too heavy a burden for it to bear.' Let us then see at what points the attack has been launched.

The source of the evidence has been attacked. Long ago Celsus urged the objection that the evidence for the Resurrection depends very largely on the word of Mary Magdalene, a half-crazed, hysterical woman, out of whom

Jesus had cast seven devils.[1] The other main source of the
evidence is Peter, a highly suggestible, impulsive, unstable,
unbalanced Galilaean fisherman, or Paul, an epileptic with
all an epileptic's penchant for seeing visions.

The contradictions within the story have been advanced.
No two Gospels list the same women as coming to the tomb.
In Mark it is Mary Magdalene, Mary the mother of James,
and Salome (Mark 16.1); in Luke it is the two Marys and
Joanna (24.10); in Matthew it is simply the two Marys.
Mark says that the women came to the tomb very early in
the morning, when the sun had risen (16.2); John says that
Mary Magdalene came, when it was still dark (20.1);
Matthew says that they came, after the Sabbath, toward the
dawn of the first day of the week (28.1). The identity of the
messenger or messengers in the tomb varies from Gospel to
Gospel. In Mark the messenger is a young man clothed in a
long white garment (16.5,6); in Luke the news is given by
two men in shining garments (24.4-6); in Matthew the
messenger is the angel of the Lord (28.2-5); in John the
message is delivered by two angels (20.12,13). In Mark and
Luke the women simply come to find the stone rolled away
from the mouth of the tomb (Mark 16.3,4; Luke 24.2); but
in Matthew the stone is miraculously rolled away by an angel
of the Lord, who came and sat upon it; and this amazing
event together with the earthquake which accompanied it
seems to have happened in the sight of the women (Matt.
28.2,3). Only Matthew has the story of the sealing of the
tomb and the mounting of a guard upon it (27.62-66), an
arrangement of which the women certainly could not have
known, or they could have had no hope of entering the tomb.

We may feel, and we may rightly feel, that discrepancies
such as we have cited are of little or no importance, but
within the Resurrection narratives there does emerge one
very real problem, the problem of fitting together the

[1] Luke 8.2; Origen, *Against Celsus* 2.55.

appearances in and around Jerusalem, and the appearances in Galilee.

Mark rightly ends at Mark 16.8, and the concluding verses are no part of the original Gospel, as any modern translation will show. There are in Mark, therefore, no actual Resurrection appearances at all. In Matthew there is a brief appearance to the women as they return to Jerusalem from the tomb (28.9,10), but the central and essential appearance, the appearance to the disciples, is in Galilee (28.16-20). In Luke all the appearances are in or around Jerusalem. There is the appearance on the road to Emmaus (24.13-35), and the appearance where the disciples are gathered together (24.36-49). Luke's narrative is further complicated by the fact that at least at a first reading the Ascension seems to take place on the same day as the Resurrection (24.50-53). But, to make Luke's evidence complete, it must be stated that the words 'and (was) carried up into heaven' in verse 51 are missing from many of the best manuscripts. Weymouth retains them; the RV notes in the margin that they are doubtful; Moffatt and the Twentieth Century New Testament enclose them in square brackets; the RSV omits them, but notes that certain manuscripts do have them. And it is also to be remembered that in Acts Luke says that Jesus was in communication with the disciples for forty days (Acts 1.3). The place of the Ascension in Luke's narrative may be doubtful; it is not doubtful that in Luke the Resurrection appearances all take place in Jerusalem, and there are none recorded in Galilee. The situation in John is also complicated. In John there are Resurrection appearances to Mary in the Garden, and to the disciples, without and with Thomas, in their meeting place in Jerusalem in John 20; but in John 21 there is the appearance of Jesus to the group of disciples by the lakeside in Galilee. But it is generally agreed that John 21 is not part of the original Fourth Gospel, but is in the nature of an appendix by a different hand.

It can at once be seen that there is a problem here. The more radical critics solve the problem by holding that all the Resurrection appearances were in fact in Galilee, and that the Jerusalem appearances are later additions and indeed inventions. How is that conclusion arrived at?

This much certainly is true—the whole New Testament narrative would lead us to expect that the Risen Christ would appear in Galilee. After the last meal together, Jesus and his men went out to the Mount of Olives, and, apparently on the way, Jesus said to them: 'After I am raised up, I will go before you to Galilee' (Mark 14.28). It has been argued, and, as far as the Greek goes, it is perfectly possible that 'go before' does not mean 'precede, go on ahead of you', but rather, 'lead you, put myself at the head of your company and be your leader'. However that may be, it is quite clear that Jesus is, as we might say, making a rendez-vous with his men in Galilee.

The Resurrection narratives would in fact confirm this impression. In Mark the announcement of the messenger at the tomb is: 'He has risen, he is not here; see the place where they laid him. But go tell his disciples and Peter that he is going before you to Galilee; there you will see him, as he told you' (16.7). With the exception that it omits the message to Peter, Matthew's account is exactly the same (28.7). All this would undoubtedly lead us to expect that the Resurrection appearances would be in Galilee, as indeed in Matthew the great appearance is. It is not entirely irrelevant that the apocryphal Gospel of Peter makes Peter say: 'We, the twelve disciples of the Lord, were weeping and were in sorrow, and each one being grieved for that which had befallen departed unto his own house. But I, Simon Peter, and Andrew my brother, took our nets and went unto the sea; and there was with us Levi the son of Alphaeus' (The Gospel of Peter 13.59,60). It has been suggested that this information of the Gospel of Peter actually comes from the lost ending of Mark's Gospel, if the original of Mark did not actually finish at Mark 16.8.

On the face of it here there is a line of tradition which tells that the disciples fled to Galilee, or that they drifted back to their trade there, and that it was there that the Resurrection appearances of Jesus took place. It is precisely this that many of the radical critics believe took place, and they believe that the Jerusalem appearances as recorded in Luke and John are later inventions, due either to certain happenings which we shall shortly examine, or due to the fact that Christian apologetic desired to have certain appearances of Jesus in the sacred city and near to the tomb where his body had been laid.

There is no doubt at all that a case can be made for the view that the Resurrection appearances did take place in Galilee.

This leads us very naturally to the next great battleground of the Resurrection arguments, the question of the empty tomb. Before we come to the way in which the Galilaean appearances view and the question of the empty tomb are connected, there are certain other things at which we must glance.

Attempts to explain away the empty tomb are as old as Christianity itself. It has been suggested that Jesus did not die on the Cross but that he swooned, and that in the cool of the tomb he revived, and then succeeded in making his escape from it. He and his disciples then claimed that he had risen from the dead, and he lived on until he died a natural death. The Gospel narratives make it very clear that Jesus did die on the Cross. The Fourth Gospel tells of the spear thrust into his side to make assurance of his death doubly sure (John 19.34). His body was lovingly handled for its anointing and embalming and any sign of life would certainly have been noticed. Even if he had only swooned, it is impossible to see how he could have disentangled himself from the long windings of the grave clothes, and how he could have opened the tomb from the inside and so escaped. If he had escaped, he would have been a broken and battered figure instead of a figure of glory. And it is hard to see how Christianity in the end could have survived the violent anti-climax of a natural death. There are very few who would nowadays take the swoon theory with any seriousness.

It has been suggested that the Jews took his body away lest the tomb where he had been laid become a martyr's shrine. But it is impossible to see how any Jew could ever have conceived it possible that one who was crucified could ever come to be regarded as a martyr of God, for the Jewish law pronounced its curse on every one who hung upon a tree (Deut. 21.23). And yet this suggestion must have had some currency in the early days, for Tertullian with grim humour speaks of the story that the gardener removed the body of Jesus 'lest his lettuces should be trampled on by the throng of visitors'.[1]

It has been suggested that the disciples removed the body of Jesus and then claimed that he had risen from the dead. That in fact is what Matthew says that the Jews feared would happen (27.63-66), and that is what the late and slanderous Jewish book the *Tol'doth Yeshu* says did happen. But it is impossible to think of the whole of Christianity being founded on a lie. It is impossible to think of the disciples preaching the Resurrection faith and dying for the Resurrection faith in the full awareness that the whole thing was a deliberate falsehood. As Joseph Klausner, himself a great Jew and scholar, says: 'That is impossible; *deliberate imposture* is not the substance out of which the religion of millions of mankind is created . . . The nineteen hundred years' faith of millions is not founded on deception.'[2]

Guignebert would explain the empty tomb by the fact that Jesus' body was never buried in it at all, but was most likely

[1] *De Spectaculis* 30. [2] *Jesus of Nazareth*, pp. 357, 359.

removed from the Cross by his executioners and flung into the pit into which the bodies of executed prisoners were thrown.[1]

Both Holtzmann and Klausner think it likely that what happened was that Joseph of Arimathaea was unwilling to give the body of Jesus anything but a temporary refuge, and that as soon as the Sabbath was ended, he caused it to be quietly removed and buried in some unknown place.[2]

But by far the most startling explanation of the empty tomb is that of Kirsopp Lake in *The Historical Evidence of the Resurrection of Jesus Christ*. Lake suggests that after the crucifixion the disciples fled to Galilee, and that it was there that they saw the appearance which persuaded them that Jesus was still alive. When they did return to Jerusalem, they found that there was a story that the women had gone to the tomb on the first day of the week and had found it empty. This was, of course, at once seized on as further proof that Jesus was still alive. But it is Lake's suggestion that the story of the women was the result of a misunderstanding. He suggests that they actually visited the wrong grave, and that a young man directed them to the right one with the words: 'He is not here; see the place where they laid him' (Mark 16.6), the words, 'He has risen', being a later addition and insertion into that verse. There can be few more astonishing suggestions than that the story of the empty tomb goes back to a mistake by a company of women which sent them to the wrong tomb, and a misunderstanding of some unknown young man's directions to set them right.

The last argument in the attempt to disprove the story of the empty tomb is the fact that it is not mentioned outside the Gospels. It is argued that, if Paul had known of it, he would have cited it as an argument for the Resurrection somewhere in I Corinthians 15, and that, if Peter had really

[1] *Jesus*, p. 500. [2] J. Klausner, *Jesus of Nazareth*, p. 35; O. Holtzmann, *The Life of Jesus*, p. 499.

known about it, he would have mentioned it somewhere in the sermon of Acts 2, especially in the section Acts 2.29-36.

The argument is, not that the empy tomb was a factor in the creating of faith in a Risen Lord, but that the appearances of the Risen Lord produced the story of the empty tomb.

We now come to the last of the debated questions in regard to the Resurrection. This is the argument as to what the appearances of Jesus after his death really were. There are three main positions.

(i)   There are very few who would deny that something happened, and there are comparatively few who would wish to explain the Resurrection appearances of Jesus in terms of hallucination, but there are many who would say that the alleged appearances of the Risen Christ were subjective visions. That is to say, they were visions seen within the mind, or thought to be seen with the eye, but with no corresponding objective reality. This idea would be explained somewhat as follows.

If we place any belief at all in the Gospel records, the disciples cannot have been entirely unprepared for the Cross, for Jesus forewarned them that it was to come (Mark 8.31; 9.31; 10.33). Yet when it came, it came with such shattering tragedy that faith and hope collapsed. Yet even in the darkest hour the disciples never stopped thinking about Jesus. In Mark 14.27 we read, as the AV has it, that Jesus said to his disciples: 'All ye shall be offended because of me this night.' The RSV translates it: 'You will all fall away.' Lagrange vividly translates it: 'You will all be demoralized.' Demoralized they were, 'for they had hoped that he was the one to redeem Israel' (Luke 24.21). But even in such a condition they were still thinking and talking of this Jesus (Luke 24.15-21).

Now, if this was so, something else was almost bound to follow in the mind of a Jew. All Jewish history showed the saints of God persecuted, oppressed and killed. All Jewish history showed the tale of a series of national disasters and national tragedies. And yet somehow out of every tragedy truth had emerged stronger and faith had burned brighter. Somehow out of the tragedy something fine had come by the action of God, something which had left God, not further away, but nearer. It was almost inevitable that the mind of the disciples should follow along this line in regard to Jesus. When they had had time to think, their whole national history and experience would predispose them to look for the hand of God even in the tragedy.

We may go a step further. The place of Peter in the Resurrection narratives is central. A special message is sent to him (Mark 16.7); one of the first appearances is said to be to him (Luke 24.34); he comes at the head of Paul's list of those by whom Jesus was seen (I Cor. 15.5). So Guignebert writes beautifully about Peter: 'We must think of him as having returned to his home at Capernaum and resumed his fisherman's calling, with the boat which had so often taken Jesus across the lake. Everything there calls up memories of those days of hope and joy. The vision of his Master pursues him and indeed fills his whole life. His entire being centres in the thought that it cannot all be ended, that something will happen and happen through him, that he has not deceived us or forsaken us, he will come back to us. And while his grief at the loss of Jesus grows, and a hope that has no form becomes keener, the expectation of the inevitable miracle surges in his heart. Reason demanded that the miracle should be a personal manifestation of the Crucified. Need we be surprised that Peter saw Jesus?'[1] 'In the inner tension and tumult of his soul,' writes Holtzmann, 'a certain idea possesses Peter unceasingly; in a moment of supreme excitement the same idea presents itself to his mind objectively also.'[2] 'There can be no question,' writes

[1] *Jesus*, p. 522.   [2] *The Life of Jesus*, p. 503.

Klausner, 'but that some of the ardent Galilaeans saw their Lord and Messiah in a vision.'[1] It is Renan who puts this most beautifully: 'It was love which resurrected Jesus.'[2]

The idea, and it is a lovely idea, is that the disciples, and especially Peter, thought themselves and loved themselves into seeing a vision of Jesus. But that vision was not objective; it was subjective. It had no objective reality; it was something which happened within their hearts. And once that experience had come to Peter, it spread like an infection and a contagion, because it is characteristic of that kind of experience to repeat itself in others.

No one will deny the beauty of this idea; and yet the line between it and downright hallucination is precariously thin. It is a vision due to a kind of self-hypnotism. The seer of it never for a moment doubted its reality—but nonetheless it was not real, but only a product of the man's own mind.

C. G. Montefiore feels bound to accept this explanation of the Resurrection experiences. Yet, he says, he has a difficulty. Then he goes on: 'It is, perhaps, less a difficulty than a sadness . . . It is hard to be content that great religious results should have had not quite satisfactory causes. The subjective vision was, in one sense, an "illusion". Yet upon this illusion hung the great religious result which we call Christianity.'[3]

Here is exactly the difficulty which anyone must feel. No one questions the reverence of this view; no one questions the beauty of the idea that an undefeatable love within the heart somehow produced its own evidence to enable it to believe that that which it wished to be true was true. But the belief in the Resurrection is the centre of the Christian faith, and, if this idea is correct, there is no escape from the conclusion that Christianity rests on a delusion, however understandable and however emotionally beautiful that

[1] *Jesus of Nazareth*, p. 358. [2] Quoted A. M. Ramsey, *The Resurrection of Christ*, p. 48. [3] *The Synoptic Gospels*, I, 399.

delusion may be. An hallucination remains an hallucination, even when it produces the very effect that one wishes to be true. If we hold that the appearances of Jesus Christ after his death were no more than subjective visions, then we can do no other than say, as Strauss said in the original form of his life of Jesus, that the disciples passed from the position, 'He must live!' to the position, 'He does live! He has appeared!'[1] And that is to say that the belief in the Resurrection was no more than self-induced and was without any basis in actual fact.

(ii) The second position is the position of Theodor Keim, which is fully, eloquently, persuasively and reverently stated in his great life of Jesus (*Jesus of Nazara*, VI, 274-365). Keim's position is that the appearances of Jesus were indeed visions, but that they were not subjective visions, but objective visions sent to the disciples by the direct action and the direct intervention of God. They were not, to use Keim's own phrases, 'human projections' but rather 'divine manifestations'.

The contention of Keim is that, if Jesus had really ended on a cross, he could never have been accepted as Messiah by any Jew, because the Law is inescapably clear that one who was crucified was under the curse of God (Deut. 21.23). To the Jew this would have been an insuperable barrier to the acceptance of Jesus as the divine vice-regent of God. 'All the evidences go to prove that the belief in the Messiah would have died out without the living Jesus; and by the return of the Apostles to the synagogue, to Judaism, the gold of the words of Jesus would have been buried in the dust of oblivion. The greatest of men would have passed away and left no trace; for a time Galilee would have preserved some truth and fiction about him; but his cause would have begotten no religious exaltation and no Paul.' What was required was, in Keim's famous phrase, 'a telegram from

[1] *Life of Jesus,* 4th edition, II, 634 ff.

heaven'. 'The evidence that Jesus was alive, the telegram from heaven, was necessary after an earthly downfall which was unexampled, and which in the childhood of the human race would be convincing; the evidence that he was alive was therefore given by his own impulsion and by the will of God.'[1]

On this view the appearances of Jesus were not subjective visions produced by love and meditation and memory; they were divinely sent objective visions. 'Even the corporeal appearance,' says Keim, 'may be granted to those who are afraid of losing everything, unless they have this plastic representation for their thought and their faith.'[2]

There is no doubt of the attraction of this view. It obviates so many difficulties. In particular it solves the difficulty of what happened in the end to the physical body of Jesus, for that physical body of Jesus simply does not enter into the matter at all. Certainly, it leaves the explanation of the empty tomb difficult, and, if the fact of the empty tomb be accepted, this view will mean that the body of Jesus was removed from the tomb by some unknown human hand. But that in many ways is easier to understand than it is to understand what happened to the body of Jesus in the end, if the Resurrection was in some sense a physical event.

But this view encounters one serious difficulty. On this view the appearances of Jesus were purely spiritual with no physical element in them at all. And yet it is true that the narratives of the Resurrection appearances in the Gospels make a great deal of the actual physical character of that event. In Mark there are no actual appearances of Jesus narrated, and so the problem does not arise. In Matthew the problem is very slight. The only physical reference in the Resurrection story in Matthew is the saying that the women returning from the empty tomb met the risen Christ 'and took hold of his feet and worshipped him' (28.9). But the

[1] *Jesus of Nazara*, VI, 362.   [2] *Jesus of Nazara*, VI, 362.

matter is very different in Luke. In Luke in the Emmaus story Jesus takes bread and breaks it with his own hands in the Emmaus house (24.30); in his appearance to the disciples he invites them to touch and handle him, telling them that a spirit has neither flesh nor bones, and thus inferring that he has; and he also shares a meal with them (24.39,41). In John there is a curious double strand of evidence, for there Jesus forbids Mary Magdalene to cling to him, and yet, when he meets the disciples, he shows them his hands and his side; Thomas, who is hard to convince, is actually invited to touch and handle him, and so to convince himself of the reality of his body and his wounds; and in the last chapter the risen Christ prepares a meal for his disciples, when they disembark from the fishing-boat (John 20.17,20,27; 21.10-13).

In Paul's account of the Resurrection appearances of Jesus (I Cor. 15.3-8) the word that is consistently used is that Jesus *was seen* by the various people involved. (The RSV needlessly and indeed wrongly substitutes *appeared*; the Greek is *ōphthē*). And in Paul there is no suggestion of touching and handling. In fact the suggestion is rather the reverse.

There is real difficulty here. There can be two instinctive reactions to this. There are some who find the continual physical references uncomfortable and unnecessary and who rather shrink from them; and there are some who find them reassuring and necessary. It may well be suggestive that the later the Gospel the more the physical side is stressed; and it may well be that the physical side of the Resurrection came to be elaborated and developed in the interests of underlining and emphasizing the reality of the Resurrection.

In spite of the physical references in the Resurrection narratives as they stand, it would still be possible to accept Keim's interpretation of divinely caused and divinely sent visions, designed and purposed and despatched by God to convince men of the continued and glorified life of Jesus.

(iii) Lastly, there is the view, which is the orthodox view, that the Resurrection of Jesus was in some sense a bodily resurrection, and was in some sense a physical as well as a spiritual event. This is the view that Jesus returned to his disciples in the body.

It is very easy to state this view, but it is not by any means so easy to define what it means. Even if we take the evidence of the Gospels exactly as it is, there remain questions and difficulties. Let us take that evidence and set it down.

(a) The appearance of the risen Christ was such as to demand worship. When the women returning from the tomb met him, they took hold of his feet and worshipped him (Matt. 28.9). When the disciples met him on the hilltop in Galilee, when they saw him they worshipped him (Matt. 28.17). The final cry of Thomas is: 'My Lord and my God!' (John 20.28). It may be that the Gospel writers depict the wounds of Christ as still there, yet in spite of that he is no figure of pathos. 'Then the disciples were glad when they saw the Lord' (John 20.20). Whatever may be said of the bodily resurrection of Jesus, the Gospel picture is that he carried the atmosphere of glory with him. The apocryphal Gospel of Peter has a good deal of information of its own about the Passion and the Resurrection—it dates to about AD 150—and it has one significant saying. The words of the messenger in the tomb to the woman are: 'Why have you come? Whom do you seek? Not him who was crucified, for he has risen and gone. But if you do not believe it, look in and see the place where he lay, that he is not here. *For he has risen and gone to the place from which he was sent*' (The Gospel of Peter 13.55,56). Whoever wrote that sentence believed that the risen Christ had returned to his glory; and therefore the resurrection appearances are appearances of the glorified Christ. This would indeed explain the atmosphere of worship; and it would indeed mean that it is not enough to speak of a bodily and a physical resurrection.

(*b*) One of the curious features of the resurrection narratives is the number of times when it is stated that Jesus was not recognized. He was not recognized by the two travellers on the way to Emmaus (Luke 24.16). He was not recognized by Mary Magdalene (John 20.14). It is clear that the disciples by the lakeside were not exactly certain that it was Jesus whom they saw (John 21.4,12). Even in Galilee some worshipped, but some doubted (Matt. 28.17). Here again we seem to come upon a bodily resurrection—and something more.

(*c*) The Gospel narratives seem to indicate that they regard the risen Christ as independent of time and space. He comes and goes, as it were, at will. The end of the Emmaus story is his vanishing from sight (Luke 24.31). The assembled disciples are terrified, thinking that it is a spirit which they see (Luke 24.37). When the doors are shut, suddenly he is in the midst of them (John 20.19,26). Once again, even taking the Gospel narratives as they stand, we seem to be in the presence of a bodily resurrection—and something more.

(*d*) We have already noted the stress on the physical side of the resurrection appearances. But it has to be remembered that even here there remains something essentially mysterious, for Mary Magdalene is forbidden to touch him (John 20.17), but Thomas is invited to do so (John 20.27).

Let us for the moment leave the matter there, and return to it later. It is enough for the moment to see that the underlying evidence of the Gospels is such as to show that it is not enough simply to talk about a bodily and a physical resurrection of Jesus and to leave it at that. There is something more.

It is worth noting that, if a Jew believed in any kind of resurrection, it would be a physical and bodily resurrection. The Pharisaic belief in the resurrection was crudely physical. In the times of the Maccabees the Jewish martyrs expected to receive back from God those very parts of their bodies which their enemies tortured and mutilated (II Macc. 7.11; 14.46).

In 2 Baruch the hope of the resurrection is that a man will be resurrected in exactly the same form in which he died. Baruch asks God: 'In what shape will those live who live in thy day?' The answer is: 'The earth will then assuredly restore the dead, which it now receives, in order to preserve them, making no change in their form, but as it has received, so it will restore them, and as I delivered them unto it, so also will it raise them' (2 Baruch 49.2-4). The hope is the hope of a physical resurrection in exactly the form in which a man died, after which will come the judgment. So far was this belief carried that it was sometimes held that a man would rise wearing exactly the same clothes as the clothes in which he had been laid in his tomb,[1] and there were many cases of dying Rabbis who gave minute and detailed instructions regarding the clothes in which they were to be buried.[2]

In view of this it is not difficult to see that the whole tendency would be to make the Resurrection of Jesus as physical as possible; the physical side of it would tend to be exaggerated.

Let us return to the radical criticism of the resurrection narratives of the Gospels.

These narratives are attacked on the ground of their discrepancies and their inconsistencies. We already noted that many of the discrepancies are quite trifling and unimportant. It might well be argued that the discrepancies are the best proof of the sincerity of the writers. No two people will ever give precisely the same account of any event. If they do, the indication is not so much an indication of truthtelling as it is of collaboration, not to say collusion. Collin

---

[1] *Sanhedrin* 90 b.   [2] W. O. E. Oesterley, *The Doctrine of the Last Things*, p. 141.

Brooks tells how on one occasion he and the famous banker Sir James Hope Simpson had to provide some specimen signatures on little cards for the block-makers to use. As Sir James signed the little cards, he turned to Collin Brooks and said: 'Brooks, if ever you want to compare two signatures, and you hold one over the other against a window or a light, and they coincide exactly—one is a forgery.'[1] Exact correspondence either of signatures or narratives tends to prove the reverse of what it is intended to prove. Even if the discrepancies are large, as, for instance, the discrepancies between the appearances in Jerusalem and in Galilee might be said to be, it is to be remembered that secular history can easily parallel this. It is a notorious fact of ancient history that Polybius, the Greek historian, and Livy, the Latin historian, represent Hannibal in his invasion of Italy crossing the Alps by completely different routes, routes which can by no stretch of imagination be harmonized, yet no one doubts that Hannibal most certainly arrived in Italy. The discrepancy is there—but so is the quite undeniable fact. Discrepancies in the accounts of the Resurrection cannot be used as evidence to prove that the Resurrection did not take place.

It is further to be noted that it was not necessary to wait until the nineteenth and twentieth centuries to find men of common sense, and acute minds, and reputable scholarship reading the New Testament. The men who wrote the New Testament were not fools. They were quite as able to recognize a discrepancy as we are! And yet they left them there, thereby showing that they certainly did not seem to them to invalidate the fact of the Resurrection.

Let us next look at the 'subjective vision' interpretation of the Resurrection. In this case it is absolutely necessary to examine the mental and emotional condition of the men who were alleged to have had these subjective visions.

[1] *More Tavern Talk,* p. 70.

Beyond a doubt the women were on their way to the tomb to anoint and to pay the last tributes to the body of a dead man (Luke 24.1,3; Matt. 28.1; Mark 16.1; John 20.2). The Gospel of Peter makes them say: 'Even if we were not able to weep and to lament him on that day whereon he was crucified, yet let us now do so at his tomb' (The Gospel of Peter 12.52). It was a dead body for which Mary was looking (John 20.13-15). For the disciples hope was dead, despair was in their hearts, and fear had them in its grip. They had hoped that Jesus would have been the one to redeem Israel —but no (Luke 24.21). The doors of the place where they were meeting were locked and barred for fear (John 20.19,25). The reaction of the women was total amazement (Mark 16.8; Matt. 28.8). The news of the empty tomb came to the disciples as an empty tale beyond belief (Luke 24.11). At the sight of Jesus they were not so much overjoyed as terrified (Luke 24.37). The news seemed to them far too good to be possibly true (Luke 24.41). They were prostrate with sorrow. The Gospel of Peter makes Peter say: 'But I with my fellows was in grief, and we were wounded in our minds, and would have hid ourselves' (The Gospel of Peter 7.26). The Gospel of Peter shows us the disciples weeping and grieved and going back to the boats because there was nowhere else to go and nothing else to do, a situation which is very probably reflected in John 21 (The Gospel of Peter 13.59,60; John 21.3).

Now in view of all this it is perfectly possible that given time, given some weeks or even months of memory and of reflection, the disciples might well have worked themselves into a state in which they read the lesson of Jewish history and saw God's purpose in disaster, but it is not possible that they should think themselves into that state overnight. If we are willing to spread the Resurrection events over, say, a year, as Renan in fact does, then the subjective vision interpretation is possible and even likely; but, if we accept the chronology of the Gospels and see the whole matter happening over a weekend, it is impossible. The subjective vision interpretation is an attempt to rationalize by a method that is itself unreasonable.

We may note one further significant fact. The Gospel narratives are far from deliberately spectacular and are far from piling wonder upon wonder. They are in fact astonishingly reticent and amazingly restrained. We can see how restrained the canonical Gospels are when we turn to the apocryphal Gospels and Acts. In the Acts of Pilate the rolling away of the stone takes place at midnight in the presence of the women and the terrified guard dazzled and blinded by the angelic lightning (Acts of Pilate 23). In the Gospel of Peter the guards pitch a tent and keep watch and there is a description of the actual event of the Resurrection. There was a great sound in heaven and two men descended from heaven, clothed in dazzling light, and approached the tomb. The stone was rolled away and knocked over on its side and the men entered the tomb. Then 'three men came out of the tomb, two of them sustaining the other, and a cross following after them. And of the two they saw that their heads reached unto heaven, but of him that was led by them that it overpassed the heavens.' And all this took place in the very presence of the terrified guards (The Gospel of Peter 9.35-42). The Latin manuscript Codex Bobbiensis (k) inserts an account of the event of the Resurrection between Mark 16.3 and 4: 'But suddenly at the third hour of the day there was darkness over the whole circle of the earth, and the angels descended from the heavens and rising in the glory of the living God they ascended with him, and straightway it was light.'

It is clear that we no sooner enter into the world of the apocryphal Gospels than we enter into the world of legend. We no sooner read them than we begin to see the reticence and the restraint of the canonical Gospels. Taken all in all, the narrative of the Gospels does not read like fiction or legend, and certainly does not pile wonder upon wonder. There are no doubt elaborations in it but its general atmosphere is an atmosphere of credibility.

What conclusions are we then to come to regarding the Resurrection of Jesus and regarding the form in which it took place?

That something happened is certain beyond all doubt; and the proof that something happened is the existence of the Christian Church. Had the disciples not been convinced that Jesus was not dead, but that he had conquered death and was alive for evermore, there would be no Christian Church today. After the crucifixion we see a company of hopeless, frightened, disappointed men, terrified that they would be involved in the same fate as him who had been their master, and with nothing but the desire to escape back to Galilee and to get back to their old jobs and forget. Fear, despair, flight—these were the things which filled the horizon of the disciples after the event of Calvary. This was their condition at the Passover time. Seven weeks later Pentecost came and we see these same men filled with a blazing hope and confidence, with a courage which defied the Sanhedrin and the mob alike. Every effect must have an adequate cause. And the only possible explanation of this astonishing change is that the disciples were firmly convinced that Jesus was alive. Seven weeks before they had been prepared to go away and forget—in which case there would have been no Christian Church. But now they are prepared to take on the impossible task of winning a world for Jesus Christ—and therefore the Church was born. And it all happened because something or some series of things had happened which convinced them that Jesus was still alive. We have only to contrast the picture of Peter denying his Master in his craven determination to save his own skin (Mark 14.66-72) with the picture of this same Peter two months later bidding the

Sanhedrin to do its worst (Acts 4) to see this astonishing change epitomized; and the cause of that change was the conviction that Jesus had risen from the dead.

Acts has justly been called The Gospel of the Resurrection, and there is not a sermon in it in which the Resurrection is not at the centre of the preacher's message (Acts 2.24,32; 3.15,26; 4.10,33; 5.30; 10.40; 13.30-34; 17.31). The Resurrection, as it has been put, had become the star in the firmament of Christianity.

It is beyond dispute that the existence of the Church is due to the conviction of the disciples that Jesus had risen from the dead. It would be very difficult to believe that the beginning of the Church and the continued existence of the Church are based either on an hallucination or on an imposture. In view of the existence of the Church it is more difficult not to believe in the Resurrection than it is to believe in it.

But we must still ask one question—even although we know before we ask it that we can never answer it fully and completely. What was the nature of these appearances of Jesus which meant so much both to those who first received him and to the history of the Church, and, therefore, to the history of the world? Have we any evidence, any guidance, which will enable us to glimpse something of the character of these appearances?

The first list of Resurrection appearances is that given by Paul in I Corinthians 15.3-8, for I Corinthians was almost certainly written before the earliest of the Gospels. For the purposes of our present quest by far the most significant thing in that list is *the occurrence of Paul's name in it*. 'Last of all,' writes Paul, 'as to one untimely born, he appeared also to me' (I Cor. 15.8). Now this is to say that Paul in no way distinguished the appearance of Jesus to him from Jesus' appearance to Peter, to the twelve, to the five hundred and to James. 'Have I not seen Jesus our Lord?' he demands

(I Cor. 9.1). This appearance to Paul took place about three years after the crucifixion, and, therefore, about three years after the other appearances which are cited. If that be so, it certainly was not a bodily and physical appearance of Jesus. The impression which the narratives of Paul's conversion on the Damascus road leave is twofold (Acts 9.1-9; 22.1-16; 26.13-19). First, it was a manifestation of blinding light and of a voice, but not a physical appearance of Jesus. Second, it was private to Paul, for the travelling companions of Paul clearly did not know what was going on (Acts 9.7). The appearance of Jesus to Paul was a quite unmistakable manifestation that Jesus was triumphantly alive, but it was not a bodily appearance of Jesus, and yet it is included without question with the other appearances.

No sooner have we begun on this line of thought than another question arises. If Paul does not distinguish the appearance of Jesus Christ to him on the Damascus Road from the appearances of Jesus as related in the Gospels, wherein do the appearances in the Gospels differ from the appearance to Stephen (Acts 7.55); the appearance to Ananias with the instructions regarding the reception of Paul (Acts 9.10-16); the later appearance when Jesus appeared to Paul in Ephesus to cheer and comfort his heart (Acts 18.9,10); the still later appearance in which the Lord appeared to Paul and assured him that he would yet reach, and preach in, Rome (Acts 23.11)? What is the difference between the appearances of Jesus as narrated in the Gospels and these appearances as related in Acts?

What is the difference between what we might call the original appearances of Jesus and the appearances to the saints in all ages? Take the case of Francis of Assisi. In his unsettlement and his unhappiness and his dissatisfaction with the fashionable life of earthly gallantry which he led, he was faced with the leper on the road. G. K. Chesterton describes the incident. 'Francis Bernardone saw his fear coming up the road towards him; the fear that comes from within and not without; though it stood white and horrible in the sunlight. For once in the long rush of his life his soul must have stood still. Then he sprang from his horse, knowing nothing between stillness and swiftness, and rushed on the leper and threw his arms round him. It was the beginning of a long vocation among many lepers, for whom he did many services; to this man he gave what money he could and mounted and rode on. We do not know how far he rode or with what sense of the things around him; *but it is said that when he looked back, he could see no figure on the road.*' And since then many have believed—as Francis believed—that it was Jesus Christ who appeared to him in that leper that day. Wherein does this differ from the appearances of the first days?

A. J. Gossip used to have two stories which he loved to tell and which none of his ex-students are likely to forget. The first was of Ramon Lull who lived at the turn of the thirteenth century, and who was once a courtier and a steward of kings, and who became a Franciscan, a defender of the faith and a missionary to the Moslems in North Africa. Ramon Lull would tell how he became what he became. Christ came to him once, carrying his Cross, and tried to place it in Ramon Lull's hands, saying: 'Carry this for me!' But Ramon Lull pushed him and his Cross away. A second time Christ came; a second time he tried to lay his Cross in Ramon Lull's hands, saying: 'Carry this for me!' and a second time Ramon Lull refused. A third time Christ came, and as Ramon Lull said: 'He took his Cross, he said no word, but with a look he left it in my hands. What could I do but take it up and carry it on?' Wherein, if in anything, does Ramon Lull's experience of Jesus Christ in person differ from the experiences which the New Testament records?

A. J. Gossip's second story was about himself, and Gossip was a saint of God. One week he had had a very busy week;

time for preparation for Sunday had been very scarce, but to the best of his ability he had done what he could. On that Sunday morning, as he mounted the stairs of his pulpit in St Matthew's Church in Glasgow, as he rounded the bend in them, clearly and unmistakably he met Christ. And Christ said to him looking at the sermon in his hands: 'Is this the best that you could do?' Knowing of the week that lay behind, humbly yet sincerely Gossip said: 'Lord, it is.' And that Sunday that hastily prepared sermon became in his hands and by the grace of God a trumpet. No one who ever heard Gossip tell that story could doubt the reality of it. Wherein does an appearance of Christ like that differ from the appearances recorded in the Gospels?

We may put the question we are asking in another form: What, if any, is the difference between the risen Christ and the ever-living Christ? I do not think that in kind there is any difference, although I think that there is a difference in purpose. The first appearances of Jesus to his own were *evidential*. They were utterly necessary to convince his disciples that the Cross was not the end but the beginning, that he was still victoriously alive. Ever since, the appearances of the risen and ever-living Christ have been *sustaining, strengthening, renewing;* but the Christ who appears is the same.

We would not say that the way of the appearance is the same. At the very first the appearances were visible to those who loved him—and only to them, with the single exception of Paul who was fighting against love—although whatever happened to the physical body of Jesus his resurrection body was more than physical. In the later days it was to the eye of faith and love that he appeared, but he did appear and still he does appear. The closing words of Albert Schweitzer's *The Quest of the Historical Jesus* still ring true: 'He comes to us as One unknown, without a name, as of old, by the lakeside, he came to those men who knew him not. He speaks to us the same word: "Follow thou me!" and sets us to the tasks which he has to fulfil for our time. He commands. And to those who obey him, whether they be wise or simple, he will reveal himself in the toils, the conflicts, the sufferings which they shall pass through in his fellowship, and, as an ineffable mystery, they shall learn in their own experience who he is.'[1]

The risen Christ and the ever-living Christ are one and the same. To the risen Christ the Church owed its beginning; to the ever-living Christ it owes its continued existence. That is why for the Christian the Resurrection is not so much an event in history, not even the greatest event in history, as a reality which has to be appropriated. And we shall find help for this act of personal appropriation, if we look at the Resurrection events, simply as the Gospels tell them, along three lines—what the risen Christ offered, where the risen Christ showed himself, and to whom the risen Christ appeared.

When the risen Jesus appeared to his followers, he offered them certain things.

(i) He offered them a *commission*. 'Go into all the world,' he said, 'and preach the gospel to the whole creation' (Mark 16.15). 'Go and make disciples of all nations' (Matt. 28.19). The commission of the risen Jesus is to go out and to make the kingdom of the world into the Kingdom of God.

(ii) He offered them a *task*. 'You shall be my witnesses,' he said, 'in Jerusalem and in all Judaea and Samaria and to the end of the earth' (Acts 1.8). The task of the Christian is to be by word and by life the witness of Jesus.

(iii) He offered them a *message*. They were to preach repentance and the remission of sins (Luke 24.47). They were to awaken men to the realization of the depth and urgency of their need, and then they were to point and lead them to the one in whom that need could be met.

[1] *The Quest of the Historical Jesus*, 3rd edition 1954, p. 401.

(iv)   He offered them *an explanation*. He opened the Scriptures to them, and showed them how these Scriptures pointed to himself (Luke 24.27; 44-46). Jesus opened the eyes of his people to the meaning of history and to the culmination of history in himself.

(v)   He offered them a *promise*. 'Lo,' he said, 'I am with you always, to the close of the age' (Matt. 28.20). 'You shall receive power,' he said, 'when the Holy Spirit has come upon you' (Acts 1.8). With the commission and the task he gave the power to carry them out.

We must now look at the places where the risen Jesus showed himself to men.

(i)   He showed himself to men in the garden *beside the empty tomb* (Matt. 28.1-8; Mark 16.1-8; Luke 24.1-9; John 20.1-18). Beside that same tomb in which they had laid Jesus with broken hearts in the bitterness of death he appeared to them in the new-born radiance of glory. And by his appearing he turned death into victory and the shadows of the night into the joy of the morning.

(ii)   He showed himself to them *as they travelled on the road* (Luke 24.13-30). When he met them, they were travelling in disillusionment; when he left them they were travelling in wonder. The road that led to nowhere became with the risen Jesus the road that led to glory. John Drinkwater wrote:

> Shakespeare is dust, and will not come
> To question from his Avon tomb,
> And Socrates and Shelley keep
> An Attic and Italian sleep.

> They see not. But, O Christians, who
> Throng Holborn and Fifth Avenue,
> May you not meet, in spite of death
> A traveller from Nazareth?

(iii)   He showed himself to men *in the cottage home* (Luke 24.28-31). It was in the breaking of bread, not a sacramental service, but in a village house that he was known to them. 'Where two or three are gathered in my name,' he said, 'there am I in the midst of them' (Matt. 18.20). And it has been beautifully suggested that the two or three are father, mother and child. The fact of the risen Jesus turns every common house into a temple.

(iv)   He showed himself *on the lakeside to men who were at their fishing* (John 21). Not in the Temple, not in the synagogue, not in any so-called holy place or sacred shrine, but in the day's work he came to them. There is a saying of Jesus, not in the Gospels but surely genuine: 'Cleave the wood and you will find me, raise the stone and I am there.' The meaning is that when the carpenter is working with the wood and the mason with the stone Jesus is there. Because of the risen Christ all work has become worship.

(v)   He showed himself to men *in the upper room*, where they were sitting in sheer terror and in bleak despair (Mark 16.14; Luke 24.36-39; John 20.19-29). He came when they had lost their courage and when they had lost their faith, and by his coming the fear was turned into confidence and the despair into hope. But one thing is to be noted—they were waiting *together* and they were waiting, as we may assume, in the *upper room* where they had companied with Jesus. We are likeliest of all to meet the risen Christ when we wait in fellowship, and when we wait in some place which has been consecrated by his presence.

The risen Jesus by his appearances banished the sorrow of death, turned every common road into the road to glory, sanctified the home, consecrated work, and defeated despair.

Finally, we must see to whom the risen Jesus appeared, and it may well be that we shall find this study the most illuminating of all.

(i)   He appeared to *love*. The accounts of the Crucifixion and of the Resurrection may differ in detail in the different Gospels, but in the centre of the picture of every one of them stands Mary Magdalene. She was there at the foot of the cross (Matt. 27.56; Mark 15.40; John 19.25). She was there when they laid Jesus in the tomb (Matt. 27.61; Mark 15.47). She was the first to be there on the Resurrection morning even before the first streaks of dawn had come (Matt. 28.1; Mark 16.1; Luke 24.10; John 20.1). In Mary Magdalene is personified the love and the devotion of one who owed everything to Jesus, and who knew it. It is of the greatest significance that the first appearance of Jesus was to one whose only claim was love.

(ii)   He appeared to *sorrowing penitence*. As far as we can work it out, the second appearance of Jesus was to Peter (Luke 24.34; I Cor. 15.5; cp. Mark 16.7). There is no shame of penitence so bitter and so deep in all the New Testament as there was in that moment when Peter after his denial of his Lord flung himself out and wept his heart out (Matt. 26.75; Mark 14.72; Luke 22.62). The astonishing thing is that Peter was there with his fellow-disciples at all. A man of lesser moral fibre would never have been able to meet the eyes of his fellow-men. Jesus appeared to Peter to save him from too much self-torture, from too much self-hatred, from too much despair. Here is enshrined the precious truth that Jesus makes a personal visit of forgiveness and of reconciliation to every penitent heart.

(iii)   He appeared to *bewildered seeking*. He appeared to the two on the road to Emmaus when they were talking of the things which had happened in Jerusalem, and when they were seeking to find some explanation for the tragedy for which there seemed to be no explanation (Luke 24.14-21). This story must be read with great care to find the full meaning of it. At first it sounds like a story of sheer despair. He in whom they had set their hopes as the redeemer and deliverer of Israel had been hounded to a cross, and it seemed that all their hopes were dust and ashes. But the whole point of the story is that *they were still talking about Jesus*. Bewildered they might be, but they could not forget.

Shattered their world might be, but somewhere at the heart of it there was still this Jesus. There are times when a man cannot understand; there are times when life is a dark mystery and when there are problems which are so immense that they defy all solution; there are times when in face of this distracted world the work of Jesus seems failure. But if at the heart of our personal world there still remains this Jesus, if he is still quite unforgettable, if he refuses to be banished from the mind and from the heart, then in the end he comes—and the darkness becomes light.

(iv)   He appeared to *utter despair and to desperate fear*. That was the attitude of the disciples in the upper room, when Jesus came back to them (Luke 24.36-41; John 20.19). Their nerves were in such a jangle of terror that they were even terrified when he appeared to them (Luke 24.37). They had reached the ultimate depths of fear and hopelessness and despair. But, as Neville Talbot put it, 'When you get to the bottom, you find God.' They had reached bottom, but they were still thinking about Jesus, they were still haunted by Jesus, he was somehow still the centre of their lives. Jesus still comes to those who even in fear and despair cannot help remembering and cannot stop loving him.

(v)   He came to *doubt*, for Jesus appeared specially for the sake of Thomas (John 20.24-29). There is doubt and doubt. There is a kind of clever doubt which takes a pride in its scepticism; there is a kind of intellectual society in which it is rather discreditable to profess anything other than agnosticism. There is a kind of comfortable agnosticism which enjoys a twilight of not unpleasant uncertainty. But there is also a doubt which is a desperate and a passionate thing, a doubt which is an agony of spirit, because it matters so much to be sure, a doubt which is a matter of life and death. That was the state of Thomas. The doubt of Thomas did not spring from the intellectual superiority which prefers not to commit itself, but from the desperate need and desire to believe. At such a time if a man continues to ask his questions, if he continues his desperate struggle for certainty, the risen Jesus will come back to him.

(vi)   He appeared to two men *who were fighting a last ditch battle against him*. He appeared to James, one of his brothers who did not believe in him (John 7.5; I Cor. 15.7); and, above all, he appeared to Paul (I Cor. 15.8; Acts 9.1-9; 22.1-11; 26.1-18). There is nothing so very surprising about this. James and especially Paul took Jesus seriously enough to hate him. Here was no vague neutrality, no serene indifference; here was flaming opposition to some one who had to be taken with immense and enormous seriousness. So long as a man takes Jesus seriously, even if he opposes Jesus to the last ditch, there always remains the chance that Jesus will break in upon him. Against indifference little or nothing can be done; but, if a man disbelieves intensely, there is still the possibility that he may yet believe equally intensely. The man who takes Jesus seriously can never tell when the risen Jesus will at last confront him and break the barriers down.

(vii)   Lastly, Jesus appeared to *the assembled disciples* (Acts 1.4-8). We may well say that this was his first appearance to his Church. When men are assembled for worship and for prayer, it is then that the risen Jesus can always appear among them.

There are few better attested facts in history than the Resurrection of Jesus. And what the risen Jesus once did, he still does. He comes in answer to love; he comes with forgiveness to the heart in penitence and shame; he comes to the bewildered yet still seeking mind; he comes when despair and fear have reached the bottom, and have still not succeeded in forgetting him; he comes when doubt is agonizing because the need of certainty is so imperative; he comes to the man who takes him seriously, even if that man hates him; he comes to his own worshipping people in his own Church.

12

THE ASCENSION

IT may be said that there is no incident in the life of Jesus at one and the same time so beset with difficulties and so essential as the Ascension.

The actual New Testament evidence for the Ascension is very meagre. The only unquestioned evidence for it is in Acts 1.1-12. It is briefly mentioned in Mark 16.19: 'So the Lord Jesus, after he had spoken to them, was taken up into heaven, and sat down at the right hand of God.' But it is quite certain that Mark 16.9-20 is not an original part of Mark's Gospel, and, therefore, cannot be taken as first-hand evidence for the Ascension. In Luke 24.51 the Authorized Version reads: 'And it came to pass, while he blessed them, he was parted from them, and carried up into heaven.' But it is a matter of considerable uncertainty whether or not the phrase 'and was carried up into heaven' is part of the original text. The Revised Version notes that it is doubtful; Moffatt encloses it in brackets; and the Revised Standard Version relegates it to a footnote. Even if Luke 24.51 was unquestionably accepted as evidence for the Ascension, the difficulty would still remain that on any natural reading of the whole chapter it seems to place the Ascension on the same day as the Resurrection and not forty days after it as Acts 1.1-12 does.

It is further strange that in certain semi-credal passages of the New Testament the Ascension is omitted, and the impression left is that Jesus passed straight from Resurrection to exaltation. In Rom. 8.34 Paul speaks of Christ Jesus who *died*, who was *raised* from the dead, and who *is at the right hand of God*. In I Cor. 15.3-5 Paul speaks of Christ who *died* for our sins, was *buried*, and was *raised* on the third day, and *appeared* to Cephas and to the others. In these passages, where we would expect a clear reference to the Ascension, we do not in fact find one.

It is nevertheless quite clear that this is one of the many occasions when it would be quite wrong to place any weight on the argument from silence. The rest of the New Testament makes it quite clear that the Ascension was an integral part of Christian belief. In the Fourth Gospel Jesus says: 'What if you were to see the Son of man ascending where he was before?' (John 6.62). In the same Gospel Jesus says to Mary Magdalene: 'Do not hold me, for I have not yet ascended to the Father; but go to my brethren and say to them, I am ascending to my Father and your Father, to my God and your God' (John 20.17). In the New Testament letters there are unmistakable references to the Ascension. In Ephesians we read: 'He who descended is he who also ascended far above all the heavens, that he might fill all things' (Eph. 4.8-10). The writer to the Hebrews speaks of Jesus as 'a great high priest who has passed through the heavens' (Heb. 4.14); he speaks of Jesus as 'exalted above the heavens' (Heb. 7.26). Peter speaks of Jesus who has 'gone into heaven and is at the right hand of God' (I Peter 3.22). In I Timothy there is part of a very early Christian hymn which says of Jesus:

> He was manifested in the flesh,
> vindicated in the Spirit,
> seen by angels,
> believed on in the world
> taken up in glory (I Tim. 3.16).

There is no lack of evidence that the Ascension was an essential part of the Christian picture of Jesus.

There is another series of passages which fit into this picture. These are the passages which speak of Jesus as being *at the right hand of God*. Jesus himself quoted Ps. 110.1, which is the basis of all these passages:

> 'The Lord said to my Lord,
> Sit at my right hand,
> till I put thy enemies under thy feet'
> (Matt. 22.44)

This is again quoted in Peter's sermon in Acts 2.33f.; cp. 3.21; 5.31; 7.56. Paul speaks of God highly exalting Jesus (Phil. 2.9), and of God setting Jesus Christ at his own right hand in the heavenly places (Eph. 1.20). He speaks of Christ sitting on the right hand of God (Col. 3.1), and of Christ as risen and at the right hand of God (Rom. 8.34). The writer to the Hebrews says of Jesus that, after he had completed his earthly work, he sat down on the right hand of the Majesty on high (1.3); he speaks of him as being crowned with glory and honour (2.9); he speaks of Jesus as the high priest who is set on the right hand of the throne of the Majesty in heaven (8.1); he speaks of Jesus enduring the cross and despising the shame, and being set down at the right hand of the throne of God (12.2). The John of the Revelation speaks of Jesus as sharing the throne of God (Rev. 3.21). It is the warning of Jesus to his accusers that they will see the Son of Man sitting on the right hand of Power (Mark 14.62). It is easy to see that there is no stratum of New Testament thought which does not picture the exaltation of Jesus, and the exaltation necessarily involves the Ascension.

We may finally note that the Ascension is clearly a part of the creed of the early Church. It is embedded in the Apostles' Creed, which may well have expressed the baptismal confession of faith in the Roman Church in the second century. Aristides says of Jesus that he went up into the heavens;[1] Irenaeus declares that it is the belief of the Church throughout the world that the flesh of Jesus was taken up into heaven;[2] Tertullian declares that it was his own belief and the belief of the Church that he who rose from the dead was carried up or taken back into heaven.[3]

However brief and meagre the direct evidence for the Ascension may be, it is certain that the Ascension is an integral part of the New Testament picture of Jesus and an essential part of the belief of the early Church.

There is still another point in which there has been difference in the interpretation of the narrative. According to the narrative in Acts there were forty days between the death of Jesus and his final Ascension (Acts 1.3). In the arrangement of the Christian year this forty days is taken quite literally, and Ascension Day falls on the sixth Thursday after Easter. But it must be remembered that in Hebrew terminology *forty days* is a phrase which is not intended to be arithmetically accurate, but which simply describes a considerable period of time. In English we use the two phrases *ten days* and *a month* to express a longer or a shorter period without confining ourselves to actual calendar accuracy. In the Bible the phrase 'forty days' is used of the period of the flood (Gen. 7.12,17); of the stay of Moses in Mount Sinai to receive the law (Ex. 24.18); and of the time of Jesus' temptations in the wilderness (Matt. 4.2). The phrase 'forty days' simply means some considerable time. In the days of the early Church the Valentinians held that there were eighteen months between the Resurrection and the Ascension; the Ophites held that there were eleven or twelve years; Eusebius mentions the belief that the length of Jesus' ministry after the Resurrection was the same as the length of his ministry before the Resurrection. We may simply say that Jesus spent a considerable length of

[1] *Apology* 2.   [2] *Against Heresies* 1.10.1.   [3] *Against Praxeas* 2.

time with his disciples between his Resurrection and his Ascension.

To the modern mind one of the greatest difficulties in the Ascension is the word 'ascension' itself. In Acts 1.11 the Ascension is described by the word *analambanein*, which means 'to take up'; in Acts 1.9 it is described by the word *epairein*, which means 'to lift up'; although the words are different, the picture is the same. The modern objection to this is that these words come from a belief which thinks of a three-storey universe, in which the earth is in the middle, heaven above the sky and therefore literally upwards, Hades beneath the earth and therefore literally downwards. It is significant to note that this very word *analambanein* is used in the Greek Old Testament about two men whose deaths were strange and mysterious. It is used of Elijah, who went up by a whirlwind into heaven (II Kings 2.11); and in Ecclesiasticus it is used of both Elijah and Enoch, who were taken up from the earth (Eccl. 48.9; 49.14). The fact is that no one writing in either Old Testament or New Testament times would think in any other way. If anyone in those days wished to describe a mysterious ending to a life which was victorious over death, there is no other way of speaking which he could use. We do not need to literalize this picture; we do not know what actually happened at the time of the Ascension. It is not the picture which is important but the truth behind the picture. The picture is only the symbolic envelope of the truth. Let us, then, after facing all the difficulties, try to think positively about the meaning of the Ascension.

It must be clear that the Ascension was an absolute necessity. It was in the first place necessary that Jesus should remain visibly with his disciples for some time after his Resurrection. That was necessary in order that they might be truly and fully convinced that he was alive, that his legacy to them was not, as some one has put it, 'dead and in-operative information', but a living presence. It was neces-sary, as Denney says, that there should be a time in which Jesus instructed his disciples in the Christian meaning of the Old Testament, in the universality of the gospel, and in the promise of the Spirit. But it is equally clear that it was absolutely necessary that that period should come to an end. Jesus could not go on making personal appearances to his men, for that would have meant that, though he truly belonged to the spiritual world, he was still limited to visible, personal appearances. Nor would it have been right that such appearances should become fewer and fewer, and so drift indeterminately and undecidedly to a close. This special time must definitely *end*, and not fade out. Some quite definite end to the interim period after the Resurrection was necessary; and Denney is right when he calls the Ascension 'a point of transition'.

Still further, something which could only be called an Ascension had to happen. A. J. Maclean points out that Jesus could not remain for ever visibly with his disciples, that clearly he could not die all over again, and that therefore the end had to come in *glorification* and not in *dissolution*. However we look at this, some terminating event had to happen, and that event is the Ascension.

From all this it is clear that the right place for the Ascension is not at the end of the story of the Gospels but at the beginning of the Acts. In one sense the Ascension closes a chapter, but in another and an even greater sense it begins a new chapter, for the Ascension is the necessary prelude to the events of Pentecost and to the coming of the Holy Spirit. The Ascension is the necessary conclusion of one part of Jesus' ministry and the equally necessary introduction to the next and even greater part of that ministry.

Still further, the Ascension is the *enthronement* of Jesus. It was, as Denney puts it, his enthroning 'in reality and not in imagination'. Jesus ascended in order to reign. As Paul has it: 'He must reign until he has put all his enemies under his feet' (I Cor. 15.25). He was raised 'far above all rule and authority and power and dominion, not only in this age, but in that which is to come' (Eph. 1.21). Jesus had to ascend into heaven to begin his universal rule and kingdom and dominion.

So far we have looked at the Ascension, as it were, from the point of view of Jesus. For him it was the transition from his ministry upon earth to his glory in heaven. It was the end of one stage and the beginning of another. It was his final enthronement after the humiliation of the Cross and the triumph of the Resurrection. But there is something in the Ascension of infinite preciousness for us also. It is the consistent belief of the New Testament that Jesus ascended to make intercession for us. It is Christ who is at the right hand of God who indeed intercedes for us (Rom. 8.34). He always lives to make intercession for us (Heb. 7.25). He appears in the presence of God on our behalf (Heb. 9.24). In him we have an advocate in the presence of God (I John 2.1). He is the mediator who stands between man and God to bring man and God together, and he continues that mediating work in the presence of God (Heb. 8.6; 12.24; I Tim. 2.1,5). Jesus ascended, not to end his work for men, but to continue his work for men, that in this or in any other world he may still carry on his ministry of intercession and mediation for men.

There remains still one other consequence of the Ascension which it may be that we can only dimly grasp and understand. It is the great truth of Christianity that the Christian shares in all the experiences of his Lord. In the Ascension the manhood of Jesus was taken up into the heavenly places, and, therefore, our manhood will also be so taken up. As Denney finely says, the Ascension is the proof that manhood is destined for heaven and not for the grave, that manhood is destined, not for dissolution but for glory. Here is the answer to the hope which Tennyson expressed:

> Thou wilt not leave us in the dust;
>   Thou madest man, he knows not why;
>   He thinks he was not made to die;
> And Thou hast made him; Thou art just.

It may be that we may end our study of the Ascension by remembering a hint and a suggestion which certain writers have reverently made. It may be that the days between the Resurrection and the Ascension were necessary for Jesus too, that it was for him a time of the increasing spiritualization of his earthly body until he could ascend to the glory of God. The Authorized Version translates John 20.17: '*I ascend* unto my Father and your Father, unto my God and your God.' But the Revised Standard Version translates it perfectly correctly: '*I am ascending* to my Father and your Father, to my God and your God.' *I am ascending*—it may well be that this means that the Ascension was not so much an event, as a process reaching to a culmination. Of this conception we can only say that we do not know whether or not it is true, but maybe we may see in it the foretaste and example of that which life should be for everyone of us—a long development through grace until in the end we too are taken up to God. It may be that we may think of this in terms of Charles Wesley's lines:

> Changed from glory into glory,
>   Till in heaven we take our place,
> Till we cast our crowns before Thee
>   Lost in wonder, love, and praise.

13

JESUS CHRIST IS LORD

IT is the experience of life that we have to live long with a person before we can know him in any real sense of the term. It is also the experience of life that the most valuable people in life are not the shallow people who carry all their goods in the shop window, but the people whose character and kindness, whose personality and wisdom grow more and more precious the longer we know them. This was necessarily the experience of the Christian Church and of the individual Christian in regard to Jesus Christ. The longer men think about Jesus the greater he becomes; and the longer they live with him the more they know that no human categories can contain him.

One of the great practical problems of the early Church was to find a name and a title for Jesus which would at least in some sense sum up what they held him to be. 'Son of Man' is an obscure title only intelligible after a study of Jewish intertestamental literature. 'Son of David' and 'Messiah' are titles immediately intelligible to a Jew, but meaningless to a Greek without a long course of preliminary instruction. 'Son of God' was a title too liable to be read in terms of Greek mythology, and too suggestive of the Greek demi-gods and of the Greek heroes who were the children of the unions of immortal gods with mortal men. But in the end the Church did find its great title for Jesus Christ, and that title is the title LORD, in Greek *kurios*. The word *kurios* occurs in the New Testament well over six hundred times, and, of these six hundred odd times, more than three hundred occur in the writings of Paul.

The application of this title to Jesus was a growth and a development. It may be said as a general rule that Jesus did not become known as *kurios*, Lord, until after his resurrection, and that after his resurrection *kurios* became the great Christian title for him.

It is unfortunate that this is a fact which the Authorized Version very badly obscures. We shall very soon go on to study the meanings of the word *kurios*; when we do so, we shall find that *kurie*, the vocative case of the word, that is, the case used in addressing other people, is the commonest of all Greek expressions of respect, and is used as 'Sir' is used in English. Many and many a time in the Gospels Jesus is addressed as *kurie*, but the meaning is far nearer 'Sir' or 'Master' than 'Lord'; and any modern translation will show this in the Gospels. To take an example, both the Syro-Phoenician woman and the Samaritan woman address Jesus as *kurie* (Mark 7.28; Matt. 15.27; John 4.11), but it is quite obvious that, meeting Jesus for the first time, they cannot be using the word in the same sense as Paul uses it after years of living with the risen Christ.

The really significant use of *kurios* is not so much when it is used in address to Jesus, in which case it need mean no more than 'Sir', but when it is used of him in narrative, when he is referred to as 'the Lord' by the person who is writing or speaking of him. This use occurs hardly at all in Mark and Matthew; it is beginning to occur in Luke and in John; but in Paul it is regular and constant. For Paul, and for the early Church in its wider aspect, Jesus is distinctively and characteristically 'the Lord'.

So much so is this the case that 'Jesus Christ is Lord' became nothing less than the creed of the early Church. It is Paul's dream, and Paul believes that it is God's dream, that a day will come when every tongue will confess that Jesus

Christ is Lord (Phil. 2.11). The confession that Jesus Christ is Lord, and the belief in the Resurrection, are necessary elements in salvation (Rom. 10.9). It is only in and through the Holy Spirit that a man can say that Jesus Christ is Lord (I Cor. 12.3). Paul does not preach himself but Jesus Christ as Lord (II Cor. 4.5). There is one Lord, Jesus Christ (I Cor. 8.6). There is one Lord, one faith, and one baptism (Eph. 4.5). The Christian in his heart must reverence Christ as Lord (I Peter 3.15). The Christian Church distilled its experience of Jesus Christ in the word Lord. The word Lord became a one-word creed, a one-word summary of belief. It is clearly an imperative duty to investigate the meaning of this word which to the Christian Church became the distinctive title of Jesus Christ. *Kurios* is a word with a wide and ascending range of meanings.

(i)   *Kurios* is the normal word of respect and courtesy in address to other people. It is the exact Greek equivalent of the English Sir, the French *Monsieur*, and the German *Herr*. In the Parable of the Two Sons the superficially polite, but actually disobedient, son answers his father's request by saying: 'I go, sir,' and the word for 'sir' is *kurios* (Matt. 21.30). This is the commonest of all uses of the word *kurios*.

(ii)   In letters *kurios* is used much as in English we use the phrase 'My dear'. The soldier Apion begins his letter to his father Epimachus with greetings to 'his father and lord' (*kurios*), as we would say in English 'My dear father'.[1] Apollinarius begins his letter home with many greetings to 'his mother and lady' (*kuria*), as we would say in English, 'My dear mother'.[2] There is one possible example of this usage in the New Testament. II John begins: 'The elder to the elect lady.' *Lady* is *kuria*, and this is most likely the same kind of address. In English it would be, 'My dear elect one'. *Kurios* is the word of affectionate and respectful greeting.

[1]   A. S. Hunt and G. C. Edgar, *Select papyri* no. 112, vol. I, p. 304.   [2]   *Select Papyri* no. 111, vol. I, p. 302.

(iii) *Kurios* very commonly means 'owner'. It is used of the owner of the vineyard and the owner of the colt (Matt. 20.8; 21.40; Mark 12.9; Luke 20.13,15; 19.33).

(iv) *Kurios* is the regular word for 'master' in contra-distinction to servant or slave. No man can serve two masters, two *kurioi* (Matt. 6.24). Earthly masters (*kurioi*) are warned of their duty to the servants and the slaves over whom they have authority, and must treat others in the constant awareness that Christ is their *kurios* (Eph. 6.5,9; Col. 3.22; 4.1).

(v) *Kurios* is the regular word for 'the head of the house-hold'. No one, says Epictetus, can come into a well-ordered household from the outside and proceed to issue orders; if he does the *kurios*, the head of the house, will speedily have him ejected.[1] The father's authority over his daughter is expressed by calling him *kurios*.[2]

(vi) In Greek legal agreements and contracts entered into by a woman, the woman is regularly accompanied and represented by her *kurios*, who is her 'guardian'. In a marriage contract Thermion, daughter of Apion, has with her her guardian Apollonius.[3] In a deed of divorce Thaesis has with her as her guardian Onnophris her step-father.[4] The *kurios* is the guardian and the protector of those whose helplessness needs protection, if their rights are to be conserved.

(vii) It can be seen from these usages of the word that *kurios* is specially and particularly the word of *authority*. It is used of those who have the right to make military decisions and to despatch troops in war.[5] It is used of the magistrate who has the authority to impose the death penalty.[6] It describes a law which cannot be broken, a

---

[1] Epictetus, *Discourses* 3.22.5. [2] Aristotle, *Rhetoric* 2.24.8 (1042a 1). [3] *Select Papyri*, vol. I, p. 10. [4] *Select Papyri*, vol. I, p. 24. [5] Thucydides 4.20; 5.63; 8.5. [6] Plato, *Critias* 120 D.

decision which is valid and binding, a decree which is authoritative, a treaty which has been ratified.[1] It is so used when it is said that the Son of Man is lord (*kurios*) of the Sabbath (Mark 2.28). The word *kurios* is a word which has the atmosphere of authority around it and about it.

Even if the meaning of the word *kurios* went no further than the stage to which we have reached, *kurios* would be a great word, but there are still three further meanings of the word.

(viii)   *Kurios* became through time the standard title of the Roman Emperor. This was the process of a growth. In the West people were hesitant to use the word of the Emperor, and the Emperor was hesitant to permit it and still more hesitant to demand it. The reason was that in the West, at least in theory, the Empire remained a democracy, and the word *kurios* had too much of the suggestion of the relationship of master and slave to be palatable. In the East it was very different. There the relationship between king and subject had always been much that of master and slave, and there the word *kurios* was early used of the Emperor. But as time went on, and in particular as the Emperor came to be regarded as a god, the use of the word *kurios* spread more and more widely, until by the time of Domitian, towards the end of the first century A.D., *kurios* was the regular title of the Emperor. It was the title which appeared at the head of laws, edicts and decrees, and which appeared on coins. It becomes very common on legal papyri in dates. An edict is dated in such and such a year—the number is missing—of Hadrianus Caesar the lord. A complaint is dated 'year 33 of Aurelius Commodus Caesar the lord'. A census return is dated 'the ninth year of Antoninus Caesar the lord'.[2] *Kurios* grew to be the accepted title of imperial majesty.

(ix)   *Kurios* came to be the word and title regularly pre-

1   Aristotle, *Politics* 1286a 24; Plato, *Crito* 50 B; *Demosthenes* 24.1; Lysias 18.15.   2   *Select Papyri*, vol. II, pp. 110,276,336.

fixed to the names of gods and goddesses. Apion the Roman recruit writes to his father Epimachus: 'I thank the lord Serapis that when I was in danger on the sea he straightway saved me.'[1] An invitation to dinner runs: 'Chaeremon invites you to dine at the table of the lord Serapis in the Temple of Serapis tomorrow.'[2] *Kurios* became more and more the word of divinity, the word which was the title of a god.

(x)   So *kurios* comes to its final step. In the Septuagint, the Greek version of the Hebrew Old Testament, *kurios* is the word which is regularly used to translate the name of God, Yahweh or Jehovah, and so *kurios* became nothing less than the name of God. In the New Testament it is so used at least one hundred and fifty times (e.g. Luke 2.9; 4.18).

Deissmann is right when he says of *kurios* that it was 'a divine predicate intelligible to the whole eastern world'.

It is now plain to see what a man ought to mean when he calls Jesus Lord, or when he speaks of the Lord Jesus, or the Lord Jesus Christ. When I call Jesus Lord, I ought to mean that he is the absolute and undisputed owner and possessor of my life, and that he is the Master, whose servant and slave I must be all life long. When I call Jesus Lord, it ought to mean that I think of him as the head of that great family in heaven and in earth of which God is the Father, and of which I through him have become a member. When I call Jesus Lord, it ought to mean that I think of him as the help of the helpless and the guardian of those who have no other to protect them. When I call Jesus Lord, it ought to mean that I look on him as having absolute authority over all my life, all my thoughts, all my actions. When I call Jesus Lord, it ought to mean that he is the King and Emperor to whom I owe and give my constant homage, allegiance and loyalty.

---

[1] *Select Papyri,* vol. I, p. 304.   [2] M. David and B. A. van Groningen, *Papyrological Primer,* p. 155.

When I call Jesus Lord, it ought to mean that for me he is the Divine One whom I must for ever worship and adore.

When we remember what this word Lord means, and what we ought to mean when we take it upon our lips, we must feel something very like horror at the glib unthinking way in which it is so often used, and we must hesitate and shrink to take it on our lips, lest the speaking of it is for us nothing less than a lie. When we remember the meaning of this word Lord, and when we remember how irreverently and unthinkingly it is bandied about in the Church, then there comes a new meaning into the saying of Jesus which Matthew hands down: 'Not every one who says to me, "Lord, Lord", shall enter the kingdom of heaven, but he who does the will of my Father who is in heaven' (Matt. 7.21).

The word Lord is a one-word creed, a one-word expression of complete devotion, a one-word expression of reverence and adoration. There is little wonder that it was the word in which the Church summed up its belief in Jesus Christ, and one of the Church's most clamant needs to day is the rediscovery of its meaning, and the cessation of the empty use of the greatest name of Jesus Christ.

So then the early Church summed up and affirmed its faith and belief in Jesus in the phrase 'Jesus Christ is Lord'. From this there emerges a question which it was entirely natural that thinking men should ask. When did Jesus become Lord? When did he enter into his Lordship? Or, to put it in a wider and more comprehensive way, when did Jesus enter into that unique relationship with God which made him Lord? To that question more than one answer was given, and to look at the various answers is to see how the reverence of the Church for Jesus increased more and more, and to see how the Church struggled to find some way in which that reverence could be not entirely inadequately stated and expressed.

(i)   Sometimes the Lordship of Christ is connected with the Resurrection. Paul speaks of Jesus as being 'designated Son of God in power according to the Spirit of holiness by his resurrection from the dead' (Rom. 1.4). Here the idea is that it was the resurrection which gave Jesus the supreme right to the title of Son of God and Lord; it was the Resurrection which above all proved and attested and guaranteed what he was.

(ii)   Sometimes the special relationship of Jesus to God is, as we might put it, dated from his baptism. At the baptism the voice which came to Jesus said: 'Thou art my beloved Son; with thee I am well pleased' (Mark 1.11; Luke 3.22; Matt. 3.17). But in Luke certain manuscripts, Codex Bezae in the Greek and Codex Vercellensis and Veronensis in the Old Latin, and certain of the early Fathers record that the words of the divine voice were: 'Thou art my beloved Son; today I have begotten thee', which indeed makes the whole saying a quotation from the coronation Psalm (Ps. 2.7). If we were to accept this reading, it would mean that Jesus was a man specially prepared and trained and equipped by God throughout the years, a man who had proved himself, and disciplined himself throughout the years, until the time had come when he was ready and fit to be specially *adopted* by God to be in a unique sense his son, and in a unique sense to do his work. This is in fact the foundation of what is known as adoptionist Christology. The basic idea is that for thirty years the man Jesus was trained and equipped by God, that for thirty years the man Jesus proved himself in the life and work of the world, so that at the moment of the baptism he could be specially adopted by God as his Son to carry out his purposes. That is in fact a view of Jesus which has always attracted some thinkers.

(iii)   Some have held that Jesus entered into his special relationship with God when he was a boy of twelve in the Temple. He stayed behind and listened to the wise men.

Joseph and Mary sought him worried and anxious; they found him. Then Mary said to him: 'Son, why have you treated us so? Behold, your father and I have been looking for you anxiously.' And Jesus answered: 'How is it that you sought me? Did you not know that I must be in my Father's house?' (Luke 2.48f.). There, it is said, Jesus very gently but very firmly took the name of father from Joseph and gave it to God, for in the experience of those days he had entered into his own unique relationship with God. It would not be argued that at that time his experience of God was complete; but it would be argued that it was at that time that Jesus first discovered it.

(iv) But instinctively men sought to push further and further back this special relationship of Jesus with God. This is the whole point of the story and the doctrine of the Virgin Birth. The aim of that story is to say that Jesus did not achieve his special relationship to God, but that he was born with it.

It is worthwhile to list the difficulties which a literal interpretation of the story of the Virgin Birth involves.

(a) Both the genealogies of Jesus (Matt. 1.1-17; Luke 3.23-38) trace the lineage of Jesus through Joseph and not through Mary. It is quite clear that the compilers of these genealogies were seeking to prove that Jesus was the son of David because he was the son of Joseph. In these genealogies Mary is never even mentioned, other than to say that Joseph was her husband (Matt. 1.16).

(b) If the Virgin Birth story be taken literally, it is difficult, if not impossible, to hold that Jesus was the son of David, for Mary was the kinswoman of Elizabeth, the mother of John the Baptizer (Luke 1.36), and Elizabeth was 'of the daughters of Aaron' (Luke 1.5). If Jesus was the son of Mary alone, he was of Aaronic and not of Davidic descent.

(c) The New Testament writers freely speak of Joseph

and Mary as Jesus' parents (Luke 2.27; 2.41). They speak of Jesus' father and mother (Luke 2.33). It is to be noted that the later and less good manuscripts change *father and mother* in Luke 2.33 into *Joseph and his mother*, and change *his parents* in Luke 2.43 into *Joseph and his mother* as the difference between the Authorized Version and the Revised Standard Version in these passages show. The changes are due to the desire of the later scribes to maintain the Virgin Birth and to avoid calling Joseph the father of Jesus. But the early writers had no such scruples. 'Is not this the carpenter's son?' is the question of the people of Nazareth (Matt. 13.55). 'Is not this Joseph's son?' (Luke 4.22). John can write about Philip calling Jesus, 'Jesus of Nazareth, the son of Joseph' (John 1.45). 'Is not this Jesus, the son of Joseph,' the people say, 'whose father and mother we know?' (John 6.42). In Mark 3.21,31-35 we find Jesus' friends and Mary among them coming to bring Jesus home because they regarded him as mad. Is it really likely that Mary would say: 'Your father and I have been looking for you anxiously', if she knew that Joseph was in no sense the father of her son? (Luke 2.48). The Gospel writers speak so very naturally about Joseph as the father of Jesus that it is difficult to think that they meant anything else than what they were saying.

(*d*) When we study the text of the New Testament, we find under the immediate surface a strong strand of thought which was at least unaware of the Virgin Birth.

There are three passages in the birth stories where this becomes clear. The Syriac Version is one of the earliest of all the versions of the New Testament, and in Matt. 1.16 it reads: 'Joseph, to whom was betrothed Mary the Virgin, begat Jesus, who is called the Christ.' The Old Latin fifth-century manuscript, Codex Veronensis, entirely omits Luke 1.34: 'And Mary said to the angel: "How can this be, since I have no husband?" ' and substitutes in its place Luke 1.38:

'And Mary said: "Behold, I am the handmaid of the Lord; let it be to me according to your word." ' This substitution completely excises the Virgin Birth from the narrative of Luke. In Luke 2.5 the reading of most of the manuscripts is that Joseph went to Bethlehem 'with Mary his *betrothed* who was with child'. But the Sinaitic Syriac, and four Old Latin manuscripts, Codex Vercellensis (fourth century), Codex Veronensis (fifth century), Codex Colbertinus (twelfth century), and Codex Corbeiensis II (fifth century), all read, not *betrothed*, but *wife*. All this is to say that in the background, and in the very early background, there is a strand of tradition which does not include the Virgin Birth.

(*e*) There is no mention of the Virgin Birth outside Matthew and Luke. There is no mention of the Virgin Birth in Paul. It is sometimes claimed that Paul does speak of the Virgin Birth in Gal. 4.4, where he says: 'But when the time had fully come, God sent forth his Son, born of woman, born under the law, to redeem those who were under the law.' But the fact is that the phrase 'born of a woman' is the regular phrase for a mortal man. 'Man that is born of a woman,' we read in Job, 'is of few days and full of trouble' (Job 14.1). 'How then can man be righteous before God? How can he who is born of woman be clean?' (Job 25.4). The phrase 'born of a woman' has nothing to do with the Virgin Birth. The fact that neither Paul's letters nor his recorded sermons in Acts ever mention the Virgin Birth is no proof that Paul did not know of it, still less that he did not accept it; but it very definitely is proof that, even if Paul did know of it and did accept it, he did not set it in the forefront of his gospel, and did not regard knowledge of it and belief in it as in any way necessary for salvation.

There is no mention of the Virgin Birth in John. Again there is a question here. Nearly all the manuscripts of the New Testament in John 1.12f. read: 'But to all who received him, who believed in his name, he gave power to become children of God; who were born, not of blood nor of the will of the flesh nor of the will of man, but of God.' But there is one manuscript, the Old Latin manuscript Codex Veronensis, which reads not 'who were born', but 'who was born'. The second half of the passage then becomes a reference not to the rebirth of the Christian but to the Virgin Birth of Jesus. It is not possible to set the weight of one manuscript against the weight of practically all the manuscripts; but we shall nevertheless see that this is a very significant reading.

(f) It may finally be pointed out that a Virgin Birth would have very serious effects on the doctrine of the total incarnation, or, as Nels Ferré calls it, the 'enmanning' of Jesus Christ; for, if Jesus was born by the special action of God in a virgin, apart altogether from the natural processes of birth, then he entered into the world in a way in which no other man entered into the world, or at least in an extremely abnormal way, and, therefore, it would no longer be possible to say that he was like us in all things. This is an argument which will have different weight with different people, but it does seem that the Virgin Birth would affect the complete manhood of Jesus.

In spite of all this the idea of the Virgin Birth appears in all the early Fathers and is lodged immovably in the earliest of the creeds.

We have set out all difficulties and the problems and the contradictions which a literal belief in the Virgin Birth entails. And now one thing emerges—*these difficulties and problems and contradictions must have been every bit as apparent to the writers of the New Testament as they are to us.* We are not the first generation to have any intelligence; the New Testament writers, and the early thinkers, were quite as intelligent as we are—*and yet they allowed these contradictions to stand.* The most vivid illustration of this is the Old Latin manuscript Codex Veronensis. Let us

remember its readings. It is Veronensis which omits Luke
1.34 and substitutes for it Luke 1.38 and so erases the Virgin
Birth from Luke. Veronenis is one of the manuscripts which
call Mary Joseph's wife instead of his betrothed in Luke 2.5.
And yet it is Veronensis alone which in John 1.13 reads the
singular 'who was born' and so is the only manuscript out
of thousands to make that verse into a reference to the
Virgin Birth!

There seems to be only one possible conclusion. The New
Testament writers were not primarily concerned with the
Virgin Birth as a literal and historic fact; they were concerned with it as a symbolic way of saying that from his
very first entry into the world Jesus was in a special and
unique relationship to God. I do not think that we are
intended to take the Virgin Birth literally; I think that if we
were intended so to do the writers of Scripture and the
compilers of the New Testament would have reconciled the
inconsistencies and would have harmonized the divergences.
I think that we are clearly intended to take the story of the
Virgin Birth as a parabolic, symbolic, pictorial, metaphorical
method of carrying the unique relationship with God back
to the very birth of Jesus, quite irrespective of whether that
birth was a virgin birth or a normal birth like the birth by
which all men enter into the world.

(v)   But we have not yet come to the end of this purpose.
We have seen how the special relationship of Jesus to God
is connected with the resurrection, with the baptism, with
his experience in the Temple as a boy of twelve, with his
birth. Then comes the Fourth Gospel, and the Fourth Gospel
pushes the unique relationship of Jesus with God back to a
time before time began. It takes it completely out of time
and lodges it in the forevers of eternity. 'In the beginning
was the Word, and the Word was with God, and the Word
was God' (John 1.1). In the Fourth Gospel we have the
culmination of the whole process, the great leap of human

thought, the great vision in response to revelation, in which the relationship of Jesus Christ the Son to God the Father is something which was before time began, which is now while time shall run, and which shall be when time has come to an end. In Jesus Christ we see the very essence and being of God in human flesh—and that is the final reason why Jesus Christ is Lord.

And so in the end we come beyond theology to wondering adoration. Our minds realize the utter inadequacy of all our thinking, but our hearts cry out with Thomas in his great discovery: 'My Lord and my God!' (John 20.28).